The Power of Gathering

THE POWER OF GATHERING

How Coming Together at Mass Renews Our Faith

FATHER PAUL FARREN

PARACLETE PRESS
BREWSTER, MASSACHUSETTS

2026 First Printing
The Power of Gathering: How Coming Together at Mass Renews Our Faith
ISBN 979-8-89348-020-7

Library of Congress Cataloging-in-Publication Data
Names: Farren, Paul (Catholic priest) author
Title: The power of gathering : how coming together at Mass renews our faith / Father Paul Farren.
Description: Brewster, Massachusetts : Paraclete Press, [2026] | Summary: "Fr Farren encourages us to come to Mass, where the father is willing us to come to share in his banquet, to share in his life, and where there is an explosion of love by God for each one of us"-- Provided by publisher.
Identifiers: LCCN 2025024919 (print) | LCCN 2025024920 (ebook) | ISBN 9798893480207 trade paperback | ISBN 9798893480214 epub
Subjects: LCSH: Catholic Church--Liturgy | Mass | Christian life--Catholic authors
Classification: LCC BX2230.3 .F37 2026 (print) | LCC BX2230.3 (ebook) | DDC 264/.36--dc23/eng/20250902
LC record available at https://lccn.loc.gov/2025024919
LC ebook record available at https://lccn.loc.gov/2025024920

10 9 8 7 6 5 4 3 2 1

Published by Paraclete Press
Brewster, Massachusetts
www.paracletepress.com

Printed in the United States of America

IN MEMORY OF MY MOTHER AND FATHER
Margaret and Packie Farren

IN MEMORY OF MY GRANDPARENTS
Peggy and Mylie Coll
&
Ellen and Philip Farren

CONTENTS

	FOREWORD	9
ONE	INTRODUCTION	13
TWO	Separated from the Mass	18
THREE	God's Longing	28
FOUR	Emptying Ourselves	39
FIVE	Filled with the Word	49
SIX	Giving Ourselves to God	59
SEVEN	The Real Presence	70
EIGHT	The Power of the Holy Spirit	80
NINE	In Holy Communion	90
TEN	God's Will Be Done	101
ELEVEN	Absorbed into the Body of Christ	110
TWELVE	Powerful Medicine and Nourishment for the Weak	121
THIRTEEN	Go Out in Holy Communion	130
	NOTES	141

FOREWORD

Important phrases, when overused, can become cliché. I suspect that among Catholics following the Second Vatican Council, the profession that the Eucharist is the summit of our lives has suffered from this kind of cliché. Even religiously apathetic Catholics are probably aware that they should care more about Mass, at least coming to the parish church once or twice per year.

A tired phrase, though, is probably not wrong. After all, it has been used enough that there must be some sense of wisdom to it that would be wise for us to hear anew. Father Paul Farren's *The Power of Gathering: How Coming Together at Mass Renews Our Faith* is the kind of personal and yet theologically sound account of the Mass that could restore to the reader a sense of wonder around the Eucharist.

How so? First, the Eucharist is central to Father Paul's life as a Catholic priest. It's refreshing to see an account of the priesthood suffused with Eucharistic joy. How often we read about the various scandals related to the priesthood. Or we hear about the power struggles accompanying ordained ministry in the Roman Catholic Church in an increasingly secularized West. In this book, you have an account of the priesthood that is not about scandal or power but ultimately about the self-giving love of the Mass itself. From his ordination, to the painful separations of the COVID-19 pandemic, to an increasingly non-Catholic Ireland, you will find a story in the pages of this book about fidelity to the Eucharistic mystery of Christ's merciful and beautiful presence in a fragile world.

Second, Father Paul is a natural teacher and communicator of the Eucharist in a way that is theologically sound but avoids the kind of doctrinal technicalities that sometimes cause lay readers to not understand the Mass or the Eucharist. Don't get me wrong: It's clear that Father Paul knows the Church's various teachings on the Eucharist around true presence, sacrifice, and the vocation to charity that comes about because of participation in the Eucharistic banquet. But he expresses this wisdom in a way that any reader can not only understand but even delight in.

For this reason, the Church needs both more priests and accounts of the Eucharist in the mode of Father Paul's *The Power of Gathering*. Such accounts take seriously the late Pope Francis's exhortation for any Catholic to share the kerygma or proclamation of faith. Father Paul's approach should give us hope that this call is not an impossible one nor is it reserved only for those super-influencer evangelists who have overtaken Catholic social media. Rather, this fidelity takes the openness to letting ourselves fall in love with Christ, and then invites us to share every dimension of that love story with the world around us.

I am grateful to Father Paul for writing his own Eucharistic love story, and I hope that the reader responds to this work by thinking about why they find themselves so attracted to the Mass.

—Timothy P. O'Malley, *Associate Director for Research, McGrath Institute for Church Life*
Academic Director, Notre Dame Center for Liturgy

ONE

INTRODUCTION

I was ordained twenty-five years in July 2022. I decided that I would write a short book on the Mass to celebrate and give thanks for the twenty-five years. However, like many things in my life it took longer to do it than I expected. This book has been in the making since 2022. Maybe it has been done in God's timetable rather than mine. I had more to learn and more to believe.

The gift of priesthood is a gift that has always pointed beyond this world for me. Of course, priesthood makes no sense within the confines of this world. It only makes sense within the context of eternal life. That was revealed to me very powerfully and painfully. When I was preparing for ordination to the diaconate in 1995 my mother was dying with cancer. I was supposed to be ordained a deacon on June 10th 1995, four days after my 23rd birthday. However, following doctors' advice, the ordination was brought forward to May 13th 1995. My mother was at my ordination to the diaconate. It was the last Mass she was at. My mother died on June 4th 1995, Pentecost Sunday, at the age of 48. Hers was the first funeral I did as a deacon.

The gift of priesthood has been blessed for me. I believe my mother's illness and death revealed so much to me about priesthood, and I know that she offered her suffering for me. I was blessed to have my father at my ordination to priesthood and for over 25 years of priesthood. His faith and love and his awareness of the call to service formed me. His accompaniment over the years gave me confidence and courage. My father had been diagnosed with cancer a number of months before my silver jubilee. Thank God he was present at the two Masses of celebration I had, in St Eugene's Cathedral, where I am stationed, and in Clonmany, which is home. They were the last two public Masses that my father was at with me.

My father's cancer was incurable. He fought a strong battle until Christmas 2022. Together with my sister and her family we had Christmas dinner, and then on the 27th of December 2022 my father went to hospital. There he got weaker each day. My father died on January 3rd 2023, the feast of the Holy Name of Jesus.

My father taught me so much in life, but even more in death. His death was miraculous. In fact, there were three miracles. Back in September 2021, a short time after my father was diagnosed with cancer, I was doing a Novena with a friend in preparation for the feast of Padre Pio. I asked my friend what we should offer the Novena for, and he said that my father would not die of cancer. We did that. When my father was dying, I had forgotten about the Novena eighteen months earlier. My father had the most peaceful death without any medication of any form for the twenty-four hours before he died. When I read the death notice the undertaker prepared for my father he had included at the end, "Padre Pio pray for us." I commented on this to my friend, saying that my father did not have any particular devotion to Padre Pio. I wondered why it was there at all. It was my friend who reminded me that our Novena Prayer had been answered. My father had no syringe driver, no morphine, and as I said, no medication at all as he journeyed towards death. The Novena worked; a miracle!

My sister and I sat up with my father the night before he died. At around midnight that night I received a message on my phone from a friend. It was a chapter of a book that he was reading that night. It happened to be about death. In the pages I read what Mary said to a visionary in Medjugorje about death. Mary said,

> Dear children, you should celebrate the death of those who are close to you with the same joy that you celebrate the birth of a child.[1]

As I read that I looked at my father breathing quietly and peacefully and thought that would be easier said than done. It might be the right thing to do but it couldn't be possible to do it. Then later in the morning just before twelve o'clock Daddy died. As I said, his death was incredibly peaceful. At the end he just tightened his shoulders in, and then from the depth of his being he breathed out one last breath. Afterwards a nurse who was present said it was such a natural death, and then she said it is as natural as childbirth. It is just the same.

I was shocked that this nurse confirmed what I had read earlier in the morning and thought it must be true, and our call is to celebrate death with the same joy as birth. This was another miracle.

The third miracle gave me the confidence to write this book, and it led me to believe more deeply in the real presence of Jesus in his precious Body and Blood. The third miracle I am convinced was a Eucharistic Miracle.

As I said, my father died just before twelve noon, and about an hour before that, with my sister and my father, I celebrated Mass. It was very beautiful and peaceful. My father was not conscious but was breathing very gently. At Holy Communion time I placed a small drop of the Precious Blood on my father's tongue. Shortly after the Mass was over the nurse who made the comment about the naturalness of death came into the room. She looked into my father's mouth. She said she was going to clean it a bit using some suction because she could see blood in it. I was shocked, and I prayed one very simple prayer. I said, "Jesus, if it is your blood, stop her." She left the room to get the suction machine. She came back and she got prepared to start cleaning my father's mouth. She had just cleaned around his lips and was going into his mouth when she stopped. She said, "I can see a change in him. I am going to stop." She did stop, and my father died a few minutes later. I have no doubt that the blood on my father's tongue was the Precious Blood of Jesus: a Eucharistic Miracle.

This book is in thanksgiving to God for the gift of the Mass, the Eucharist, the Precious Body and Blood of Jesus. It is in thanksgiving to God for the gift of priesthood. It is in thanksgiving to God for the gift of my parents, and for them, by their lives and most especially their deaths, pointing my focus beyond this world.

When we look at the altar and we see a glimpse of heaven, perhaps the question shouldn't be *Why should we go to Mass?* but *Why would you not go to Mass?*

TWO

Separated from the Mass

"This breaks my heart, because all of my priesthood to date has been spent trying to get more and more people to come to Mass, and yet I can't do that today at a most critical and dangerous time."

I spoke these words on the Third Sunday of Lent 2020. It was the Sunday before St Patrick's Day. Even then we were still hoping to have daily Masses with congregations of up to one hundred. However, the next day or so that was wiped out as well. There were going to be no congregations at all—nobody in the Church for Mass. Then, a short time after that, the doors of the Church were closed. The Church was locked. It was the most awful and desperate time.

The first lockdown was incredibly difficult. We were terrified. We were angry. We began to lose all our confidence. We became afraid of one another. You see, we weren't allowed out. We really weren't allowed out. We were locked in the house. I remember when I would be coming back from the cemetery after a funeral I'd drive through the centre of the city just to look around me. It was the only time I was allowed to be there, and of course everything was closed. All the shops were closed, and there was no traffic in the middle of a weekday. It was awful, and the Church remained locked. People couldn't receive Holy Communion. They couldn't get to Mass. We never thought it was going to be like this, and when it *was* like this, we thought it would only be for a short time.

Then there were the funerals. The wake and the funeral traditionally are so powerful and so important. People gather, they tell the story, they remember, they pray. All of that was gone. There was no gathering. There was nobody there to tell the story. We all prayed on our own.

Even as someone was dying, they couldn't be physically accompanied by their family. Their families were separated from them, unable to go into the nursing home or the hospital. I remember so clearly a man telling me at his father's funeral,

> I visited my father every single day, and then for the last six weeks of his life when he needed me most, I couldn't be with him.

It was heartbreaking, and it was truly devastating. I had to use FaceTime to pray with someone with dementia who was dying. It was desperate. Then at the funerals only the immediate family could come. There were ten or twenty-five people present. Children couldn't be at their parent's funeral. Grandchildren couldn't be at their grandparent's funeral. It was all about separation and distance.

Then there were the funerals, at the beginning, of those who had died with Covid. They were horrific altogether. Their bodies couldn't be brought into their homes or into the church. They couldn't leave the hearse. That couldn't happen. On a number of occasions, we brought the bodies to the church door. There we prayed and we sang hymns, to try as best we could to give dignity to the one who had died and some comfort to those who were grieving.

We can never forget the pain and the isolation and the separation, particularly of those early days of Covid. Yet, even in the middle of it all, new ways of being emerged. We had the webcam. All of a sudden, this little camera far in the distance in the gallery of the Church became the window to the people for the priest and the window to the altar for the people.

The awareness of our connection, our communion with one another and with Jesus took time to grow. Initially when I was saying Mass in the empty church it was so difficult. There was nobody there. We are not supposed to say Mass without a congregation. They were very lonely times, and the church was a very lonely place. It was very lonely to celebrate Mass. There was a tremendous sadness.

Then over time I became more and more aware of the red light on the webcam. The red light indicated that it was working. Focusing then, I became aware of the people present, not physically present, but present from their own homes or wherever. I knew that more and more people were beginning to become aware that the Church was present to them, yes, in a very different way, but present nonetheless. Older people who had vowed that "That internet will never come into this house," got the internet and got the Mass on their television screen. They learnt a whole new language and a whole new way of being.

Then a community began to form. It was an old community and a new community. It was a community of local people and people from all over the world. What was wonderful too was that it was also a community of people from here who are now living all over the world. This community started to engage with us. This happened through Facebook and email and the telephone. We started talking to each other, and we became aware of who was present and how many were present. We also became aware of how fragile our communication was. If the internet went down or the webcam didn't work, we were lost. We depended on this fragile connection to keep us together.

We were also so conscious that by inviting people into the Church through the webcam and Facebook, we could give them a rhythm to their lives in a time of desolation, fear, and separation. We put on something every couple of hours so that prayer could carry people through the day. It gave a focus and an awareness that nobody was really on their own.

We had joy in the middle of it all, and we had massive engagement at times. I remember on the Saturday morning of the St Therese Novena, we were celebrating Mass for the Dead. We asked people to send in the names of their dead, and we would light a candle for them at St Therese's statue. We lit so many candles that during the Mass the candelabra went on fire!

So, abnormal life continued, and obviously the obligation to attend Sunday Mass was lifted. People were not obliged to attend Mass because it wasn't possible for people to attend. We need to look at the concept of an obligation to attend Mass. It is about an obligation to receive that greatest gift known to humanity. It is about an obligation to receive the gift of God physically present. It is an obligation to share fully in the life of God, in his

Precious Body and Blood, here and now. It is an obligation to receive the gift of heaven, here and now, on earth. It seems strange that there needs to be an obligation, that there is not a burning desire for all of this that would drive us to the altar every day. You could ask why there is a need for an obligation at all when we realise what is happening. I used to say that if I were Pope for the day, I'd lift the obligation to attend Sunday Mass! I wouldn't do this because I didn't think it was important. I'd do it because it is so important that people should desperately desire to go of their own accord without being forced. However, perhaps the obligation exists to reveal the vital necessity it is that we be at Mass. If that is the case, the Pope is right to keep it! The obligation is not to force people to Mass, but it reveals the absolute necessity to receive the precious Body and Blood of Jesus. It reveals the necessity of hearing the Word of God proclaimed in the community. It reveals the necessity to be sent out as the Church to be the presence of Jesus in the world. It also reveals the desire, and more than the desire, the *command* of God to keep holy the Sabbath Day.

This command of God is found in the Word of God. The Word of God is not an opinion. It is not just a good idea among other good ideas. The Word of God is the definitive word. It is the most powerful word. The Word of God is true, and the Word of God is alive and active. It will achieve what it says. We read in the book of the prophet Isaiah,

> The word that goes from my mouth does not return to me empty, without carrying out my will and succeeding in what it was sent to do. (Isa. 55:11)

So, the Word of God is not a document for debate. We are called to discern the Word and submit to the Word of God. We are called to give in to the Word of God and to accept it in its entirety. This is certainly not a modern way to be, and it is countercultural in many places today. We like to discuss, and we like to debate, and we like to decide for ourselves. However, the Word of God is not dependent, nor can it be shaped or changed by our opinion, even if it is a majority opinion. It is this Word that is proclaimed every time we celebrate the Mass.

So, if you ask why it is important that we be at Mass, the simple and first answer is that God has commanded us to keep holy the Sabbath Day. There is no way that we can keep the Sabbath any holier than being at Mass, than sharing physically in the life of Jesus. By not being at Mass, by not keeping holy the Sabbath Day, we break God's commandment.

But now we have an extra, modern question that never needed to be asked before. That question is, *How do we be at Mass?* You see, everybody is called and commanded by God to be at Mass. But *How do we actually be present at Mass?* is a new question. The webcam has enabled us to be at Mass from the comfort of our own homes. We can sit on the sofa rather than the pew now! Is this okay? Is this the way it can be now? Do we need or not need to be physically present in the church?

During lockdown, when we had no option, celebrating Mass from home enlarged our world. We became part of something bigger than ourselves. It was a wonderful gift, and it continues to be a wonderful gift for those whose health does not allow them to come to the church for Mass. Spiritual communion is a wonderful gift too, when we can receive Jesus spiritually into our lives when we are unable to receive him physically into our lives.

However, as we emerge from Covid, the bizarre truth is, what enlarged our world during lockdown has the potential to shrink our world during freedom. What do I mean by that? In lockdown we were physically separated from nearly everybody, from all others including family members and dying family members too. We made do with whatever form of communication and connection we could get. Now that freedom has returned, if we choose not to physically interact with our family, then we shrink our world to smaller than it was before Covid.

It is the same with God and the Mass. We made do with the webcam because without it we would have nothing. We would have been totally isolated. We had to accept spiritual communion because we couldn't have physical communion. Now, as freedom emerges, if we don't go from the sofa to the pew, if we have the strength and health to do so, then we are shrinking our world to fit ourselves. If we are fit and able, nothing is a substitute to being physically present at Mass and to receiving the Precious Body and Blood of Jesus.

When we do this, we enlarge our world. I believe that the evil spirit always wants to shrink our world. He wants to make our world just the size of ourselves. That makes us individualistic. It makes us separate and self-focused. This has been the philosophy of the Western world for so long. It is a philosophy that denies the reality of death and makes us believe that we are going to live in this world for ever.

When we share in the Precious Body and the Precious Blood of Jesus, we share in his life, and therefore our world becomes the size of his world. Our world becomes eternal, and we break through the division between heaven and earth. So, we are taken out of ourselves—out of control of our lives—and we share in the eternal life of God.

You see, in a wonderful and modern way, when we were locked in the house, Jesus came to us because we were prohibited from going to him. That is different now. We are free to go to Jesus, and he is waiting for us—more than waiting, he is searching for us and desperately desires that we go to him and physically share in his eternal life.

The separation that existed during lockdown can continue to exist if that is what we choose. It is certainly not what God chooses. God wants a physical union with us. That is why Jesus gave us his Precious Body and Blood at the Last Supper. The Last Supper was a physical event. The Last Supper was a meal where Jesus gathered his closest friends around the table. In a sense, it was the family gathering together. Jesus wants to gather us, his family, physically around the table for the Eucharist, to give himself to us. That is what he wants to give us every time we celebrate Mass. At Mass we don't receive a symbol. We receive Jesus, body, blood, soul and divinity. There is nothing virtual about this! It is disciples gathered around the table. It is family gathered around the table.

THREE

God's Longing

> We had wanted you and waited for you, imagined you and dreamed about you and now you are here no dream can do justice to you.[2]

These are the words of Fergal Keane, the BBC correspondent, writing a letter to his newborn son, Daniel Patrick, in 1996. They are powerful words, and they capture that longing and dreaming and imagining that parents must have as they await the birth of their child. Then there is the arrival of the child. The reality is so much more than the dream or the imagination could ever create. It is to marvel at the newborn baby. It is to look with wonder and awe at this beautiful creation, this beautiful human being. It reveals a welcome that comes from an explosion of love. It is an uncontainable love. It is a love that can't stop looking at the baby, that can't stop holding the baby, touching the baby.

> We had wanted you and waited for you.

To be wanted and waited for and then to receive an explosion of love—this is the most wonderful welcome at the entry into the world for those babies blessed to enter into such an expression of love, wonder, and awe.

Another place where you often see explosions of love is at airports. Christmas is a wonderful time for people to come home and be met at the airport by parents who have waited and dreamed about a time the family would all be together again. In some ways, the parents can react as if they are seeing their baby for the first time. Even if the child is now a grown adult, their parents can't stop looking at them, maybe stroking their face, holding them, touching them. It is a welcome home, and it is wonderful.

The opposite is awful, and it happens too. It is the times when we are not welcome and the places that don't want us. It is that feeling that nobody cares and nobody notices. Fr Peter McVerry, the Irish Jesuit priest who has worked all his life with those who are homeless and those with addictions, consistently says that the primary thing that the homeless need is not a house. It is to have someone to care for them, someone to love them, someone to want them. How often, as we walk along the street, do we avoid making eye contact with the person who is homeless or maybe inebriated with alcohol? We don't want to look at them. We don't want to engage with them. We certainly don't want to hold them or touch them. There is no explosion of love here. It is an explosion, perhaps of fear, but certainly of rejection. There is no meeting in this case. There is avoidance.

God never avoids people. He always meets them or desires to meet them. Jesus even waited in the garden of Gethsemane to meet those who would kill him (John 18:4–8). He didn't avoid them. One of the greatest moments of meeting—an explosion of love—is in the story that Jesus told about the Prodigal Son (Lk. 15). This is a wonderful story that reveals the desire and the love of God. It is a story that reveals the cost of love and the explosion of love. The cost of love was the father watching his son leave, knowing that what his son was doing was wrong, knowing that he wouldn't see his son for a long time, knowing that his heart was breaking with pain and sadness.

This brokenhearted father waited and waited and waited for his son to come home. He stood outside and watched every day for his return. I have no doubt that the father wanted his son, waited for his son, imagined his son coming home and dreamed about it. Unlike Fergal Keane, who knew he would see his son in nine months, this father didn't know when or if his son would come home.

Then he saw him. He saw him coming in the distance, a broken, hungry, poor man. But he didn't see a broken, hungry, poor man. The father saw his son, his boy, his beautiful boy. He didn't see the dirt on his face or on his clothes. He wasn't stopped by the smell. No, the father ran out and he hugged his son. He embraced him. He held him. Yes, he made eye contact with him. Yes, he stroked his face. Yes, he held him, and he kept touching him. Perhaps one of the reasons he kept doing this was to make sure it was all true. This was his son, and he had come home, and the story of his being away didn't matter. He was home. All the dreaming and all the imagining could not come close to describing the emotion of this moment. It was an explosion of love. The explosion engulfed the son. All the pain and all the sadness of the father disappeared the first moment he caught sight of his son coming home. The welcome home must have been overwhelming for the son.

A wonderful image for us coming to Mass is the image of the Father waiting on us. He is out looking for us before every Mass. He is waiting to see us in the far distance. He is willing us to come and share in his banquet, to share in his life. Every time we come to Mass we end the Father's waiting on us. Every time we come to Mass there is an explosion of love by God for each one of us.

Coming to Mass, then, is not our initiative. It is our response to God's waiting, God's willing, God's desiring, perhaps even God's need. Yes, God's need—and what do I mean by God's need?

God is the all-powerful God. God has no need at all. He is completely self-sufficient. He could tell the sky to fall today and it would fall. He has the power to do whatever he wills. With all that power, God has chosen to be vulnerable before us. There is a fascinating passage in the book of the prophet Isaiah. In the passage God says,

> With heaven my throne
> and earth my footstool,
> what house could you build for me,
> what place could you make for my rest?
> All of this was made by my hand
> and all of this is mine—it is the Lord who speaks.
> But my eyes are drawn to the person
> of humble and contrite spirit
> who trembles at my word. (Isa. 66:1–2)

God has chosen to depend on us, who tremble before the enormity and the abundance of his love, to respond to his love, to respond to his desire, to his waiting on us to come and share in his life in the Mass so that we can go from the Mass and be his presence and his love in the world. God has such respect for the gift of free will that he has given us. He won't go out and drag us home—drag us to the altar—but he will wait. He will humbly wait.

So it is vitally important in our relationship with God that we think about God before we think about ourselves. We need to think about God's emotion, God's desire, God's feeling, before we think about ourselves. So often when people explain to me why they are not going to Mass, the reasons are all their own. They tell me they don't have to go to Mass. They have their own relationship with God. They have their own spirituality. They say they don't like Mass. It doesn't suit them. It is dull. It is boring. It's not relevant to their lives. It gets in the way. The time doesn't suit. They don't like the priest. They don't like some people in the congregation. They have problems with the Church. And so the list goes on. But there is something common in all of these reasons. They are all self-focused. But what about God? Do we ever think how this impacts on God? Is it okay to leave him standing and waiting with a broken heart as we go off to do our own thing, knowing that he will be there if we want him anyway. Do we take advantage of the vulnerability of God?

Being aware of the emotion and the feeling and the desire of God has the potential to change our lives.

Often we don't engage with this, and we can think that God is beyond emotion. However, there is no scriptural evidence that God is beyond emotion. In the Old Testament we are faced often with the anger of God. Jesus reveals the emotion of God. He revealed his anger when he cleansed the temple (Matt. 21:12–17). When faced with the death of Lazarus, his friend, Jesus wept. We are also told he was moved with pity (John 11:33–35). In the Garden of Gethsemane, he was filled with anguish (Lk. 22:44). Our God is an emotional God, and our actions effect God's emotions. When we become conscious of God's emotions, our lives can be transformed.

I was given evidence of this from a person who was addicted to pornography. He told me that one day he was in a church, and he was focusing on a leaflet that had the face of Jesus on it. In a moment of intense prayer, it was revealed to him the sadness of God when people engage with pornography. He realised the devil uses pornography to taunt and torture God. He said that he felt God's pain, and he was ashamed that he had caused God such great offense with pornography. In that moment he was freed from pornography. It really was miraculous. Reflecting on what happened, he said,

> My caring for God freed me from
> pornography.

When we put the care of God and the emotion of God and the desire of God before everything else, we receive miracles. This is never truer than when we end his waiting by responding to his invitation to share in his life in the Mass.

So, we respond to the invitation and the desire of God when we go to Mass. The initiative belongs to God. God desires that we all be there. He desires that nobody be excluded. Our God is not a selective God or a God who excludes. God loves each one of us with a unique love and a unique expression of that love. Nobody is ever excluded from the love of God. Therefore, God waits for everybody. For God there are never enough people present until everybody is present. He will wait for you and he will wait for me, even if we are the furthest away and the last to come.

This comes to the heart of a very important question. That question is, *Who should come to Mass?* The answer is simple, because the answer is *Everybody*. Everybody is welcome and everybody is desired, and God waits on everybody. The Mass is not for the virtuous and the sinless. The Mass is for everybody. One of the reasons for this is that we don't own the Mass. It is not our Last Supper. It is the Last Supper of Jesus, whose life we are called to share in. We have no control over who comes to Mass. We have to realise that God waits for everyone, not just the ones we think he should wait for. There is no space for the attitude that would tell God,

> You can start now—don't be bothered waiting on the others: I'm here and my group is here.

There is no space for a self-focused attitude when it comes to going to Mass.

Jesus tells us, when the Scribes and Pharisees complained about who he was eating and drinking with,

> It is not the healthy who need the doctor, but the sick. I did not come to call the virtuous, but sinners. (Mk. 2:17)

Jesus makes it even clearer when he talks about who we should invite if we are having a lunch or a dinner. He says,

> No; when you have a party, invite the poor, the crippled, the lame, the blind; that they cannot pay you back means that you are fortunate, because repayment will be made to you when the virtuous rise again. (Lk. 14:13–14)

Then to make it clearer, again Jesus tells the story about the person who organised a great banquet, but all those he invited made excuses and didn't come. However, rather than cancel the banquet or change the time, the person sent out to the streets and the alley, to the hedgerows and the open road, and invited everybody. And the banquet went on without those who were first invited (Matt. 22:1–14).

This is very important. The banquet goes on whether we are there or not, even though we should still always miss those who are not there. The banquet, the Eucharist, the Mass are not put on to suit us. It is us suiting God. It is us responding to his invitation. It is us bringing an end to God's waiting. But the banquet goes on, and those who are present share physically in the life of God, and those who are not, don't.

This is our choice, and we do have a choice. To put it starkly, our choice is to leave our Father waiting or end his wait. His waiting is a waiting full of longing. It is like Fergal Keane. He is longing for us. He is imagining the moment he sees us. He is dreaming about the embrace when we come. Often, however, unlike Fergal Keane waiting for the birth of his son, God waits with a broken heart, a heart full of sadness, and his waiting is marked by the torture he feels at the devil's taking control of his children.

So, is it important that we go to Mass? It is more important than anything else, because it brings joy to God's heart.

FOUR

Emptying Ourselves

So, God wants us, and he waits for us, and he longs for our coming—our coming to his banquet, our coming to share in his life. Our arriving, our responding to his call, to his invitation, brings joy to God's heart. He invites us all. He wants us all at the banquet, all around his table. We know that he sends out to the highways and the byways to ensure that the banquet is full, that there is a wonderful celebration.

But there is something very strange in the parable of the wedding feast in Matthew's Gospel (Matt. 22:1–14). As we know, when nobody who was invited to the wedding feast came, the king sent out to the crossroads in the town and invited everyone to the wedding—so yes, everybody was invited. However, when the king came in to look at his guests, he noticed there was a man there who wasn't wearing a wedding garment. The king went to him and asked him how he got in, and he was silent. Then something very dramatic happened. The king said to those working at the wedding feast.

> Bind him hand and foot and throw him out into the dark, where there will be weeping and grinding of teeth. (Matt. 22:13)

This seems to be an incredible response and a complete overreaction. People had rejected the king's invitation to his banquet. Those present were probably invited at the last minute. They were there because the king wanted the banquet filled. Now he was enforcing a dress code. Should he not be grateful that the man was there without fussing about what he was wearing? What is happening here? What is Jesus telling us in this parable? Where is the fixation about the wedding garment coming from? What does the wedding garment symbolise in this parable?

Jesus doesn't mind what we wear. He doesn't judge by external appearances, so it is not about our clothes. The wedding garment is a symbol of our attitude and our lives. The man who came to the banquet without the wedding garment came on his own terms. He wasn't choosing a new life or a different life. He was wedded to his own life. At the banquet he wasn't coming to share in the life and the joy of the king. You could question why he was there at all. We are told that the wedding garment is a symbol of

> . . . a converted life full of good deeds. Sinners are invited but expected to repent.[3]

This comes to the heart of how we are to respond to God's invitation to his banquet, to share in his life at Mass whether we are on the first invitation list or just standing at the crossroads. How do we come to Mass? Do we come in our own clothes, or do we wear the wedding garment? In other words, do we come in self-focused or God-focused?

Who we are primarily focused on is at the heart of the Penitential Rite at the beginning of Mass, that time when we confess that we have sinned, that time when we ask God for mercy. Lord, have mercy. Christ, have mercy. Lord, have mercy. What does that mean?

It was St Paul who said,

> Now we are seeing a dim reflection in a mirror; but then we shall be seeing God face to face. (1 Cor. 13:12)

I read a reflection on this which said,

> What St Paul is telling us is that it is necessary for us to fade and fail. Our perfection comes when I have nothing left. We hand everything over to God and then we get to see him face to face.[4]

We have to fade and fail. In other words, we have to lose control of life. We have to surrender everything and, in a sense, to be totally empty in order for God to enter into and take over our lives.

This is what happens at the beginning of Mass. We have a number of images here. We need to take off our lives, and particularly our sinful lives, in order to put on the wedding garment of God's mercy. Another way of putting it, another image, is that we need to empty ourselves of everything, and in particular, our sinfulness, in order for God to fill us. If our lives are full there is no space for God, no openness to God.

At the beginning of Mass, we need to empty ourselves of our sinfulness. Our sinfulness blocks access for God in our lives. We need to eradicate the sinfulness to allow God in. Often, we do this in the Sacrament of Confession, a most wonderful sacrament that can renew the Church and the world. We also empty out our sinfulness at the beginning of Mass so that we have the capacity within us to receive God into our lives.

The young son, in the story of the Prodigal Son, came home empty. He had lost everything. He had committed all the sins. His appearance and his words confessed to his father that he had nothing to give him, only his sorrow and his repentance. However, what the young son gave to the father was space for the father to engulf him with his love.

I believe one of the reasons that the number of people coming to Mass is decreasing in the Western world is that we struggle to acknowledge our sinfulness. We fill ourselves up with the world and with worldly thinking, and therefore we have no space for God. We manage to do this—and it is a subtle action of the devil—by convincing ourselves that God's Word and God's law are out of date, or worse, that God will just accept the way we do things and in so doing make all our actions morally neutral. When we no longer name our sin, then we can't empty ourselves of that sin. When we don't empty ourselves of our sin, then we have no space for God.

What is a sin? Look at the Ten Commandments. Look at the two great Commandments of Love. They don't change. It was a sin in the time of Moses to take the Lord's name in vain, to steal, to kill, to commit adultery. These are still sins today. We are still called to love God first and our neighbour as our self. These commandments don't change. If we truly want to receive God into our lives at Mass, we need to get rid of the clothes of sinfulness and be clothed in the mercy of God. We need to empty ourselves of sinfulness so that God can fill every part of our life and our body with his presence.

Pope Francis, when he was speaking about Jesus's getting into Peter's boat to teach the people, remarked that the boat was empty (Lk. 5:1–11). If you remember, Peter and the Apostles had been fishing all night and had caught nothing. Peter came to shore disappointed. Life wasn't the way he wanted it to be. He felt himself to be a failure. And often, our sinfulness, if we acknowledge it, makes us feel we are failures. But what does Jesus do with Peter's disappointment? He gets into the empty boat. If Peter's boat weren't empty, Jesus could not get in. Pope Francis says,

> This is what the Lord loves to do—the Lord is the Lord of surprises—to climb into the boat of our lives when we have nothing to offer him; to enter our emptiness and fill it with his presence; to make use of our poverty to proclaim his richness, of our miseries to proclaim his mercy.[5]

So, when we come to Mass, when we respond to the invitation of God to share in his life, when we end God's waiting, we need to have space in our lives for Jesus to enter in.

It is a radical reality to come with nothing before God. Yet to be perfect is to have nothing left. It is to hand everything over. Then we see God face-to-face. Ultimately this is what happens when we die. We can take nothing with us when we die. We can own the whole world, and yet when we die our body is contained in a coffin and the coffin is contained in a grave. When we come to Mass and we plead for God's mercy, we are actually pleading with him to empty us.

If we go back to the prodigal son, he is the image of how we are to be at the beginning of Mass. He came home a beggar. When he left home he took the wealth of half the farm with him. He left a rich man in the eyes of the world. Materially, he had everything he could want. We know that he squandered it all, and he lived a life of absolute impurity. Then we are told that he came to his senses. He realised the reality of his life and he realised he had excluded his father. He went home a beggar, in rags. Everything was gone. Everything the world could give him was gone. He had nothing, only the burden of his sinfulness, his selfishness, his self-focus. When his father saw him, he recognised the rags as the wedding garment. The father, we are told,

> Ran to the boy, clasped him in his arms and kissed him tenderly. (Lk. 15:20)

In this loving embrace he removed the burden of his son's sinfulness, and he replaced it with his tender love. It is only the Father who can empty us and remove all the burdens that block his love. However, we need to be open to allowing him to do that. If we don't fall before him on our knees in repentance and allow him to embrace us, we can never be emptied. As I said, that emptying comes in the Sacrament of Confession and at the beginning of Mass. We need to celebrate the Sacrament of Confession regularly to be free and to have the space for God to inhabit our lives and our bodies. Regular Confession is vital to enter fully into the celebration of the Mass.

Without Confession we can be present at the banquet, but God can still be waiting on us to come home. If we don't regularly confess our sins, we will not be open at the beginning of Mass for God to enter in.

This is exactly what happened to the elder son in the story of the Prodigal Son. He had no space for his father's love. He couldn't kneel before his father. He didn't have that humility. He didn't have that awareness. He was blocked. He was full of bitterness. So he stood in judgement over his brother. He condemned him. He refused to share the banquet with him. In refusing to share the banquet with his brother, he rejected his father's love.

Many times, we can come to Mass, but we don't have any space for God. We can be so caught up with ourselves and with who else is there and what they are doing or not doing. We can sit in judgement over those present, and we can even say it is a scandal if they receive Holy Communion. I will come back to this later.

The older brother was so blind with bitterness and legality that he couldn't recognise his father's love. He saw his father's act of love as an act of betrayal. The older son wasn't focusing on his father. He was focusing on himself, and in so doing he was more than happy to list out his brother's sins. Today in certain areas of the Church, there seems to be a habit of focusing on and naming the sins of others. At no time in the Gospel does Jesus ask us to talk about others and name their sins. In fact, it is quite the opposite when he tells us to take the plank out of our own eye before we tackle the splinter in our sibling's eye (Matt. 7:3–5).

The Penitential Rite at the beginning of Mass is a moment for us to focus on the mercy of God, and in light of God's mercy to allow ourselves to acknowledge our sins, not the sins of others. It is a moment for us to take responsibility for our own sinfulness, for all the blockages we have to the presence of God in our lives and to the mercy of God in our lives. We pray,

> I confess to almighty God and to you, my brothers and sisters, that I have greatly sinned.[6]

We don't pray, "I confess that they have greatly sinned." When we focus on God's mercy and our need for that mercy, it is not to tell God how wonderful we are and how much better we are than anybody else. It is the moment when we strike our breast and say,

> Lord, be merciful to me, a sinner. (Lk. 18:13)

It is the moment when the older son becomes the younger son, and we realise that we are the prodigal son. None of us has the right to take our place at Mass. None of us is worthy to be at Mass. We are not at Mass because of how good we are. We are at Mass because God is merciful. God is so merciful that he forgives us. He is our Father. He has been waiting on us. He runs out to us, and in our poverty and our repentance he sees the wedding garment. If we fall before him as beggars, he empties us of all that blocks him in our lives. Because our God is so humble, we bring joy to his heart by accepting his gift of mercy and forgiveness.

FIVE

Filled with the Word

One of the most cynical parts of war is the manipulation of information. We are told at the beginning of the war between Ukraine and Russia that the Russian people were not told about what was really happening in Ukraine. The news was being blocked. They were given a completely different narrative. In modern language it would be called fake news. In many ways fake news is a phrase that is used to describe lies. Fake news is not the truth. It is lies. The first evidence of this in human history is with Adam and Eve. The serpent told them lies. The serpent contradicted God. The serpent told Adam and Eve,

> No! you will not die! God knows in fact that on the day you eat it your eyes will be opened and you will be like gods, knowing good and evil. (Gen. 3:5)

It was fake. He told them lies, but they were lured by the lies into believing that they would become gods themselves, able to decide between good and evil. We know the lie was found out because when Adam ate from the tree he hid from God. When God asked him why he was hiding Adam said,

> I was afraid because I was naked, so I hid. (Gen. 3:10)

Adam and Eve ate from the tree because they believed the fake news that they were going to become gods themselves. Then the truth dawned on them that they were nothing without God.

When we come to Mass and during the Penitential Rite we empty ourselves of our sinfulness, in some sense we become naked before God. However, the call is not to hide in our nakedness but to open ourselves to God.

This begs the questions, What are we open to in our lives? Whose voice do we listen to? When we are empty, what do we fill ourselves with? Do we listen to fake news, or do we listen to Good News?

After we empty ourselves at the beginning of Mass we listen to the Word of God, to Good News, to the readings. But do we really? What voices do we hear and respond to in our lives? Even around religion and faith and the Good News, is there fake news that we can be attracted to? Pope Francis, when speaking about fake news and the role the activity of the devil has in spreading fake news, said,

> The strategy of this skilled "Father of Lies" (Jn 8:44) is precisely mimicry, that sly and

> dangerous form of seduction that worms its way into the heart with false and alluring arguments.[7]

We can see false and alluring arguments pertaining to religion and faith today. We can see how the father of lies uses compassion as an argument to convince us that there are no consequences to our actions and that there is no destination for our lives except heaven. The father of lies wants to convince us that hell doesn't exist, so we can take heaven for granted. When we believe this and live out of that belief then the Word of God, the Good News, loses its power in our lives. Do we listen to the Good News, the Word of God, or do we listen to fake news that enables us to manipulate the Word of God to suit us?

When we are emptied of our sinfulness, what Word are we waiting to listen to? Are we open to the Word of God undiluted? We wouldn't need God's Word. We wouldn't need Jesus if we had no choice but to go to heaven. We wouldn't need direction, guidance, and accompaniment on the road if there was only the one road and the one direction. It would not be necessary. We wouldn't need a Saviour. However, Jesus tells us he is

> The way, the truth and the life. (John 14:6)

We must decide if we want to follow him. We have a choice to follow Jesus or not. If hell didn't exist, we would have no choice. Hell is the place where God is not present.

> Because those who are there are deprived of the vision of God. (CCC 633)

God allows hell to exist so that we have the choice not to be with him for ever. If we don't want to be in the presence of God, God will not force us. If we do want to be in the presence of God, our actions will reveal our desire. The prodigal son wanted to be in the presence of his father, so he went home. He knew where his father was, and he went to him. His actions revealed his desire. If we want to be in the presence of God for eternity and see him face-to-face, then we need to come to where he is physically present in this world, which is at Mass. Why would we want to be in his presence in the future when we have an opportunity to be in his presence here in the present moment and we don't take that opportunity?

When we come to Mass and when we have been emptied of our sinfulness, the first thing that begins to fill us is the Word of God. We listen to the readings from the Old Testament, the New Testament, and the Gospel. The Word of God reveals to us who God is, who we are, how we live in this world sharing in the life of Jesus, and how we journey to heaven, God's plan for us. The Word of God is the most important Word that has ever been spoken in human history and that ever will be spoken in human history.

When we bring a child to be baptised, that child is claimed for Jesus by the sign of his cross. At the beginning of the baptism ceremony the priest, the parents, and the godparents trace the sign of the cross on the child's forehead. Just before that happens the priest names the child and says,

> The Christian community welcomes you with great joy. In its name I claim you for Christ by the sign of his cross.[8]

Once the child is welcomed into the Christian community, the Body of Christ, and is claimed for Christ by the sign of the cross, the first thing that happens is that the Word of God is proclaimed. As soon as a person is claimed for Christ, to share in the life of Jesus, the Word of God is proclaimed. The Word of God is proclaimed because it is this Word that will lead them and guide them in their lives to keep them alive in Jesus. It is the Word of God in its entirety that reveals the action and the love of God and our response to that love. The Word of God proclaimed at Mass draws us into a deeper and deeper relationship with God. As we share in the life of God through his Word we share in his eternal life, and we make our journey to heaven to be with him for ever. In the Book of the Prophet Jeremiah we read that God says to Jeremiah,

> 'Before I formed you in the womb I knew you;
> before you came to birth I consecrated you;
> I have appointed you as the prophet to the nations.'
> Then God put out his hand and touched my mouth and said to me:
> 'There! I am putting my words into your mouth.' (Jer. 1:5, 9)

In the Mass, God puts his words into our mouth, into our hearts, into our souls. Through his Word he communicates his call, his plan for our lives. God has a unique plan for each one of us. Henri Nouwen says,

> God loved you before you were born, and God will love you after you die. In Scripture, God says, "I have loved you with an everlasting love." This is a very fundamental truth of your identity. This is who you are

> whether you feel it or not. You belong to God from eternity to eternity. Life is just a little opportunity for you during a few years to say, "I love you, too."[9]

The Word reveals that we belong to God for all eternity and that our time in this world is a small part of our eternal life. In this time on earth when we respond to God's plan and dream for our lives, we are expressing our love for God, our desire to share in his life, and our longing to be with him for ever in heaven. Mother Gilchrist, a Trappist nun from Norway, when life wasn't working out the way she wanted, had a profound realisation of God's plan for her. She responded to this realisation by praying,

> Jesus, I praise and thank you for the miracles and wonders you work in my life and for your perfect plan for me.[10]

Even in the most difficult times, if we keep hearing the Word of God proclaimed at Mass, we can have trust and confidence in the reality that God has a perfect plan for our lives. That plan will lead us home to heaven.

The Word of God proclaimed at Mass during the readings is God speaking directly to each one of us. We read in the letter to the Hebrews that

> The Word of God is something alive and active: it cuts like any doubled-edged sword but more finely: it can slip through the place where the soul is divided from the spirit, or the joints from the marrow; it can judge secret emotions and thoughts. No created thing can hide from him; everything is uncovered and open to the one to whom we must give account of ourselves. (Heb. 4:12)

It is the Word of God that calls us to accountability. It is the Word of God that calls us to responsibility. It is the Word of God that reveals good and evil to us—right and wrong to us. The father of lies, through mimicking God's compassion, can try to lure us to believe that we can decide what is right and wrong in our own lives, but this is fake news. We can't. It is God who reveals this. It is God's Word that enables us to live in the light. It is God's Word that enables us to be the light in the world. It is God's Word that joins us together in his body, as his presence. It is God's Word that keeps us on the way to heaven and not isolated and in free fall into the abyss—in that place where God is not present.

I once received the most beautiful description and experience of the Word of God in our lives.

If you can imagine there is a river of light that flows through this world. That river is made up of individual lights all travelling together. Each light is a soul on the journey to heaven. Jesus tells us,

> You are the light of the world. (Matt. 5:14)

When we allow the Word of God to fill our souls, each one of us becomes the light of the world. All the souls together create a wonderful river of light. They know where they are going, and there is great joy because they know their destination. Even though they cannot see her, all the souls in the river of light know that Mary is waiting for them at the entrance to heaven. Everywhere else apart from the river of light is the great abyss, that great darkness of nothingness, where there is no anchor, where there is no direction, where there is no light. It is the place to hide as Adam hid, because he knew he was naked and had nothing outside of God. But the river of light is so different because we are together in the river and flowing gently towards heaven.

What is causing us to move—what is causing us to flow towards heaven? This is probably the most wonderful part of this description and experience. What is causing the flow to heaven is like reeds—papyrus—gently swaying, and so moving the souls along together. This papyrus is the Word of God. It is the Word of God that gently flows us to heaven.

This is exactly what happens to us at Mass. The Word of God gently directs us, moves us, and flows us to the altar, where we experience heaven on earth. The Word moves us together, as community, as the Body of Christ, because God has an individual and unique, perfect plan for each one of us. God calls us to live that plan, not on our own as disconnected individuals, but as the Body of his Son, the river of light on the way to heaven.

Why is our presence necessary and vital at Mass? It is necessary and vital so that we can hear the Word of God together and allow that Word to flow us through this world as the light of Jesus for all the world to see. In the words of the Psalmist,

> O that today you would listen to his voice,
> harden not your hearts. (Ps. 94:8)

When we allow the Word of God to flow us towards heaven we have hearts of flesh, not hearts of stone, and we are open to receiving the Precious Body and the Precious Blood of Jesus.

SIX

Giving Ourselves to God

In August 1996 I went to Washington, DC, to continue my studies for priesthood. It was my first time to leave Ireland for anything but a short holiday. The day I was going we had to leave the house at about 3:30 a.m. for the flight. My family and a few friends were gathered in the house the evening before. During the evening my father got a phone call about a neighbour who was in distress. The neighbour would only agree to go to hospital if my father brought him. My father left his home and his family on that evening, the evening before his son went to America, and he cared for his neighbour and took him to the hospital. He gave his time and that precious evening to another.

For the most part we like to be in control of our lives, of our timetable. We like to do what we want. In many ways we try to own our lives. We say, "It's my life." We try to claim and declare ownership of our lives. I was at a conference during the Year of Faith in 2013. It was a conference for Post Primary teachers. At the beginning of the conference, I sat beside a friend of mine. On each chair was a small piece of paper with a piece of Scripture on it. I read the piece of Scripture that was on my chair. I took an instant dislike to it. It was from St Paul's first letter to the Corinthians. It read,

> You are not your own property, then; you have been bought at a price. (1 Cor. 6:20)

I reacted to this quotation. I showed it to my friend, who agreed that she didn't particularly like it either. There was an empty chair next to her, so she swapped my piece of Scripture for the piece on the empty chair. I can't remember what that piece of Scripture was, but I was happy with it.

The conference began with a time of prayer. The person leading us in prayer told us that the piece of Scripture that we found on our chair was an individual gift from God for each one of us that day. It was God speaking to our heart. Immediately after this was explained, my friend, sitting beside me, took away the piece of Scripture she had given to me and gave me back the original one. She smiled as she did it!

Why did I react? Why did I not want that piece of Scripture? I think that the answer is somewhere around power and control. I want to be in control of my life. I want to have power over my life. Yet St Paul tells us we have been bought and paid for. This can sound oppressive, but nothing could be further from the truth. Yes, we have been bought and paid for, but we have been bought and paid for by Jesus. Jesus did this so that we could be free. He bought us out of slavery to free us. He has bought and paid for us with his blood on the cross. No, we are not our own property. We belong to God. We are his. He made us, but he has gifted us with the gift of free will. When we are our own property, we belong to the world. When we belong to the world, we are not free. When we belong to God, we are free.

This is very important when we come to the offertory at Mass. In many ways up to this point in the Mass, God is doing for us. He is waiting for us to come home. He is emptying us through his forgiveness. He is filling us with his Word. When we come to the offertory we begin to respond to the action and the love of God. It is the moment we are called to give ourselves along with the bread and wine, in the bread and wine, to be changed and transformed into the Body of Christ. It is the moment when earth offers itself to heaven, for heaven to come down and to fill it with physical Divine Presence. The offertory of the Mass is our time to give. It is when we give ourselves and our lives to the one to whom they belong. God has called us. God has waited on us. God has freed us by emptying us of all that blocks us from him. He has filled us with his Word, and now we have the opportunity to respond to the Word that has been given to us. We take that opportunity when we give our lives back to God with the bread and wine.

This is why our presence at Mass is necessary and vital. It reveals to God that we have come to give ourselves to him. Many people who don't come to Mass give as a reason for not coming that they get nothing out of the Mass. But before we even think about what we get from the Mass we need to ask what we are willing to give in the Mass. People often choose to come to Mass when they are having difficulties in their lives, and that is marvellous and wonderful. In many ways they come to receive peace. But this still begs the question: What do we give at Mass? What is our offering? Are we there simply to receive, or are we willing to give?

Are we willing to put ourselves out for God, willing to give ourselves to God? This brings us back to my father the night before I went to America. Are we willing to leave our programmes and our plans and offer our lives to God? Our offering is at the heart of the Mass. I wonder if this is a reason a lot of people don't come to Mass. We want to keep our lives to ourselves and do what we want. If you come to Mass and enter into the full truth of the Mass, you cannot hold on to your life. That is not possible. You give your life to its owner. You give your life to God. At the offertory of the Mass our action should reflect the words of the Prayer of Abandonment written by St Charles de Foucauld. St Charles prays,

> Father,
> I abandon myself into your hands;
> do with me what you will.
> Whatever you may do, I thank you:
> I am ready for all, I accept all.
> Let only your will be done in me,
> and in all your creatures—
> I wish no more than this, O Lord.
> Into your hands I commend my soul:
> I offer it to you with all the love of my heart,
> for I love you, Lord, and so need to give myself,
> to surrender myself into your hands without reserve,
> and with boundless confidence,
> for you are my Father.

At the offertory we abandon ourselves into God's hands so that he can do with us whatever he wills. We offer him all the love of our hearts, and we surrender ourselves into his hands without reserve and with boundless confidence. We do all this not to a distant unknown God; we do it to our Father, God, Abba Father.

This is exactly what the prodigal son did. He literally surrendered himself into his father's hands. He abandoned himself to his father to do with him whatever he wanted. If you remember what the son decided he was going to say to his father, he said,

> I no longer deserve to be called your son; treat me as one of your paid servants. (Lk. 15:19)

When we surrender ourselves to God, when we abandon ourselves to God, it can only be a moment of profound humility. That humility comes from our awareness that we are deeply blessed by God's accepting our offering of ourselves. We must always remember that even though it brings the greatest joy to God's heart when we surrender ourselves to him, the gift is the one given by God to us when he accepts us.

We offer ourselves in our lowliness and in our need and in our inadequacy. Like the prodigal son we offer ourselves to God, aware that we have nothing to give him, only what he has given us. The prodigal son didn't come back to claim honours and position. He didn't even come back claiming his blood relationship with his father. He came back happy and grateful to be treated as a servant.

That is the attitude that we need to bring to the offertory of the Mass when we offer ourselves to God with the bread and wine. We come, aware that

> We are merely servants: we have done no more than our duty. (Lk. 17:10)

We shouldn't be looking for rewards, honours, or praise when we come to Mass. We should be profoundly grateful that the Father is waiting on us, and in his humility is opening himself up to our accepting the offering of ourselves.

Then just look at what the father does. He ignores his son's plea to be treated as a servant, and he treats him like royalty. There is an excited and enthusiastic reaction of the father. The father says,

> Quick! Bring out the best robe and put it on him; put a ring on his finger and sandals on his feet. Bring the calf we have been fattening, and kill it; we are going to have a feast, a celebration. (Lk. 15:24)

It is such a wonderful, loving, and emotional reaction from the father when his son comes home and offers himself back to his father. It is marvellous. We can say that we certainly don't get that reaction when we offer ourselves to God at the offertory of the Mass. However, is that true? What happens after the offertory of the Mass?

We enter into the great Eucharistic Prayer, during which the bread and the wine become the Precious Body and Blood of Jesus. At the beginning of the Eucharistic Prayer, this great prayer of thanksgiving, we are called to lift up our hearts, to lift them up to the Lord. We are called to give God thanks and praise because it is right and just. Then the reality of where we are in the Mass is revealed. This reveals one of the great mysteries of the Mass.

After we offer ourselves to God, where does he bring us? He doesn't treat us as paid servants. He clothes us with the robe of royalty, and he claims us as his own. He brings us out of time and into eternity. When we celebrate Mass, in some sense we are taken from this world and we join with the communion of saints and angels in heaven. This is a great, great mystery. The words before we pray the "Holy, Holy" are so important. These words reveal where we are and whose company we are in. An example of these words is the following:

> And so, with all the Angels and Saints, we praise you, as without end we acclaim . . .[11]

In the Mass, heaven and earth are united in praising God. We are in the company of the angels and saints in praising God. We are with them. We are all praising God using the same words at the same time. We are all praying,

Holy, Holy, Holy Lord God of hosts.
Heaven and earth are full of your glory.
Hosanna in the highest.
Blessed is he who comes in the name of the Lord.
Hosanna in the highest.[12]

I have a wonderful sense during the praying of the "Holy, Holy" that we are truly praising God for creation, for heaven and earth. We are praising him, clothed in the white robe of baptism, with all the saints and angels, hands in the air. We are praising God for the beauty, the wonder, and the colour of creation on earth, in the universe, and in heaven. Then in the second part of the "Holy, Holy" it is as if Jesus, the one who comes in the name of the Lord, reaches down and lifts me up, catching my arms raised up and throwing me into the air and catching me. The sky is so blue, and Jesus's face is so full of joy. When he catches me, he holds me gently and softly against his cheek.

In the "Holy, Holy," together with all the angels and saints, we are adoring God in his holiness. We are praising God for his glory seen in heaven and on earth. We are praising Jesus, who came to bring us home. Together we are saying, "Hosanna in the highest." Save us now. Together with those who have gone before us we acknowledge God as the one who saves us. While we praise God together, with all those on earth and in heaven, we are recognised by God, each one of us specifically and uniquely, and we are loved and held by God.

It is wonderful to realise that all of heaven is praying with us, and we are praying with them. We are praying with those who are seeing God face-to-face now and for all eternity. We are joined with them. We are one with them, and God is looking at each one of us as if we were the only person he ever created.

This is where the Father brings us when we offer ourselves to him in the Mass. He brings us into the communion of saints and angels. He brings us into his tender embrace. At the beginning of a Funeral Mass, I always say that we are never closer to those who have died than when we are at Mass. It is here in the Mass that heaven and earth meet. Just maybe, as our loved ones brought us to Mass in the past and we knelt beside them and heard their whispered prayers, when we come to Mass after they have died we can still be with them. We can still be together, not focusing on each other, but praising and adoring God together.

At their funeral Mass we prayed,

> Saints of God come to their aid,
> come to meet them, angels of the Lord.
> Receive their soul and present them to God
> the most High.[13]

In some way, in the mysterious love of God, that is what the saints and angels do for us during the Mass. They come to our aid, and they are like the servants who dressed the prodigal son. They dress us for the wedding feast, and they present us to God the Most High.

Why is it necessary and vital that we come Mass? We come to make a physical offering of ourselves to God. It can be like my father leaving our family gathering the night before I went to America. We put God first. We allow him to create our plan and our programme. We come to Mass to surrender ourselves back to the one who has bought and paid for us—the one who gives us freedom. We come to Mass so that we can join the angels and saints in praising God. We come to Mass to experience the unity of heaven and earth. We come to Mass so that God can reach down and lift us up and hold us gently and tenderly to himself.

SEVEN

The Real Presence

The first time I visited Fatima, I didn't really like it when I was there. I preferred Lourdes. Even comparing Marian Shrines can't be right, but I did back then. Of course, Fatima is completely different to Lourdes. Fatima has received a lot of attention in the recent past. It was Our Lady of Fatima who asked that Russia be consecrated to her Immaculate Heart and that we be faithful to the first Saturdays.[14] The messages of Our Lady of Fatima, messages of peace, purity, and penance, the call to pray the Rosary every day, these messages are so relevant and necessary for today.

The year before Mary appeared in Fatima, the children, Francesco, Jacinta and Lucia, experienced other apparitions. These were from the Angel of Peace. In the third apparition of the Angel of Peace in 1916 the children had a profound Eucharistic experience:

> Suddenly they felt enveloped by an intense light and rising saw the Angel holding in his hand a chalice with a Host suspended above it, from which a few drops of blood fell.[15]

This was a very dramatic experience for these young children to have. When we think about Mass and the consecration, we don't tend to think about drops of blood coming from the Host. What do we think about the real presence of Jesus? What does it mean? What does it mean to say that Jesus is really present at the consecration of the Mass? This brings us to the heart of the Mass, literally to the *heart* of the Mass. The Catechism tells us that

> The Eucharist is the source and summit of the Christian life. (CCC 1324)

The consecration of the Mass is the source and the summit of the Eucharist. It is that moment during the Eucharistic Prayer when our words give way to the words of Jesus. It is that moment when Jesus says at the Last Supper,

> This is my body. . . . This is my blood.
> (Matt. 26:26–28)

After the words are spoken, the Precious Body and the Precious Blood of Jesus are shown to the congregation. At the consecration of the Mass, the bread and the wine become the Body and the Blood of Jesus. We are told that Jesus is present, Body, Blood, Soul, and Divinity. He is fully present.

The Word of God has flowed us to the altar. We have offered ourselves to God in the bread and wine at the offertory. The bread and the wine are the fruit of the earth—the wheat and the grapes. They are also the work of human hands, so the bread and the wine are the gift from God, the fruit of the earth, and our collaboration with God, the work of human hands. This is what is changed into the Body and Blood of Jesus. Through what we offer to God he reveals his presence to us. He makes his presence real and physical. He gives us his body and his life for us to go out and be his body and his life.

We need to stop and look at what is his body and what is his life that he gives us in the Mass, that become present on the altar at the consecration. Perhaps today we can take the Body and Blood, the life of Jesus, the presence of Jesus for granted. Maybe reverence for the Body and Blood of Jesus has been lost in places today. Do we really see Holy Communion as the Body of Christ? Perhaps we just see it as a symbol of Jesus giving himself to us, but not really Jesus. Do we see it as blessed bread or holy bread, but still just bread nonetheless?

There is nothing in this world that can come close to describing what happens at Mass. Nobody in this world can make what happens at the consecration happen. It is not possible. Yes, we can offer the bread and wine to God; yes, the priest can say the words of consecration; but it is Jesus who acts and makes what happens happen. St John Chrysostom says,

> It is not man that causes the things offered to become the Body and Blood of Christ, but he who was crucified for us, Christ himself. The priest, in the role of Christ, pronounces these words, but their power and grace are God's. This is my body, he says. This word transforms the things offered.[16]

So, this is not a symbol, this is the action of Jesus and the presence of Jesus. He gives us his Body and his Blood, his life. It is the Last Supper and Calvary on the altar. God gives his body and life to us and for us. This can be so clearly witnessed in the story of the Prodigal Son, when we think of the father who waited as God waits for us; he waited for his son to come home. When his son did make the journey home, the father ran out, and he gave him his body and blood, his life, in his embrace.

Before the son went away, the father gave him all the material possessions that would have been due to him when the father died. He asked for and got his inheritance early. At that time the son thought that this was everything, all he could hope for or get. However, all material things pass away and always leave us disappointed. When the son came home, the father ran out to meet him, and in the meeting he gave him his body and his life. The father opened his arms in a moment of complete vulnerability. He wrapped his arms around his son in a complete offering of his love and his presence and his acceptance. He kissed him tenderly, and I would say that was the kiss of life he gave him—the kiss of new life.

The father didn't start by giving him a symbol of his love. He didn't give him a material gift; the gifts came afterward. The father gave himself, his body, in the embrace, and his life in the kiss. If we see Holy Communion as simply a symbol or holy or blessed bread, then this is simply a material gift. It may be very beautiful and very precious, but it is still just a material thing like many things which are the fruit of the earth and the work of human hands.

But Jesus didn't give us a material thing. He gave us his body and his life. Every time we celebrate the Mass, we celebrate Jesus's giving us his body and his life. We receive the embrace and the kiss of God. We receive the Body and the Blood of Jesus, real and present.

This can be very difficult for us to understand, to believe, and to accept. It can be so difficult for us because after the consecration the Body and

Blood of Jesus look the same as they did before. In a world of science and evidence and proof many would say that they cannot be anything other than bread and wine, and therefore, they are at best a symbol. However, what the Angel of Peace showed the three children in Fatima wasn't a symbol. The Angel showed them the Host with Blood dripping from it into the chalice. The children received the Host and the Blood.

Many people can get uncomfortable when we start speaking about blood and flesh. In some ways we can try to sanitise the Eucharist. We can try not to think about the physicality of it all. Maybe we try not to think about the physicality of Calvary either. However, we lose so much when we adopt this attitude. At the heart of what we lose is what Jesus gives to us in the Mass.

It is interesting that close to Fatima, in Santarem, there was a Eucharistic Miracle. In the thirteenth century a woman went to a witch, a fortune teller, who told her that she could cure her husband of being unfaithful if she brought her a Host. The woman received Holy Communion and took it out of her mouth and wrapped it in a veil, and almost immediately the Host started to bleed. That night she put the bleeding Host in a trunk in her bedroom. And during the night a bright light came from the trunk, and she and her husband prayed for forgiveness. That Host is still in the Church of the Holy Miracle in Santarem, and its authenticity has been declared by the Church.

When I made my trip to Fatima I didn't go to that church because, incredibly, I wasn't that interested in Eucharistic Miracles then. I am ashamed to say that now! It was Saint Carlo Acutis who introduced me to Eucharistic Miracles. Saint Carlo was a young boy who had tremendous faith in the Eucharist. He called the Eucharist his highway to heaven. He believed absolutely and completely in the real presence of Jesus in the Eucharist. His mother, Antonia Acutis, says,

> Carlo spent a lot of time in worship of Jesus, truly present in the tabernacle. He stayed there in silence, as though he were immersed in an intimate and personal dialogue with the Lord. He said that he liked to spend time in that place, which was special because "he looks at me," he explained, "And I look at him. That gaze is enriching. I let God observe me, to dig deep inside me, to form my soul, to mould it. He is truly present, not an invention. He's there. And if everyone could realize that, how they would run to it! If everyone believed in this truth, how their lives would change for the better."[17]

Carlo, even though he was just in his early teens, researched all the Eucharistic Miracles in the world. He set up a website of every Eucharistic Miracle. He documented over one hundred Eucharistic Miracles in about twenty countries in the world. Eucharistic Miracles are described as

> . . . miraculous divine intervention that are aimed at confirming faith in the real presence of the body and blood of the Lord in the Eucharist.[18]

They are miraculous divine intervention. They are pure, extravagant gifts from God to call us into a deeper faith in Jesus, present in his Body and Blood. People can be sceptical about these miracles; however, in the modern world the space for scepticism has been greatly reduced because of science. This point is very clearly made in relation to the Eucharistic Miracles that happened in Buenos Aires in the 1990s.

In the Church of St Mary in Buenos Aires on the feast of the Assumption in 1996, a Host was dropped and left on the floor until a person noticed it, picked it up, and gave it to the priest. The priest put it in water to dissolve it and placed it in the tabernacle. However, the Host did not dissolve, and when it was brought out of the tabernacle again, it was bleeding. It was flesh. Pope Francis was the archbishop of Buenos Aires then, and he had the flesh scientifically examined. One scientist was given the flesh to examine but not told where it came from. His findings are incredible. He said that the flesh came from the left side of the heart and that the patient had suffered a lot. He explained that it was obvious that the patient had certain moments when he couldn't breathe, and the oxygen couldn't reach him. The heart was inflamed. The scientist said that the patient suffered much because every aspiration was painful. He also said, quite incredibly, that the flesh of the heart was alive when he received it, because the white blood cells were still pulsating. This usually stops about fifteen minutes after the flesh is taken from the body. This scientist, Professor Frederick Zugibe, from New York, couldn't believe it and was deeply moved when he heard who owned the heart tissue.

The scientific evidence for this miracle is beyond question even to the cynics of the world. This is a miraculous intervention by God in our day that has been scientifically proven. It reveals to us what we are called to believe at the consecration of the Mass. The bread and the wine become the Body and Blood of Jesus. This is Jesus at the Last Supper, on the cross on Calvary giving us his body, giving us his blood, giving us his life. This is the embrace and the kiss of God. This is the presence of God. It is not a symbol. It is not something earthly that has been blessed and made holy. It is the real presence of Jesus.

As I said before, at Mass, heaven and earth unite. We are taken out of time, and we enter eternity. As St Peter tells us,

> But there is one thing, my friends, that you must never forget: that with the Lord, 'a day' can mean a thousand years, and a thousand years is like a day. (2 Pet. 3:8)

When we celebrate Mass, all of eternity becomes one moment—the moment Jesus gave his life, his Body and Blood for us. The bread that was broken at the Last Supper is the same bread that is broken every time we celebrate the Mass. The wine that is poured is the same wine. The life that is given on Calvary is the same life that is given every time we celebrate the Mass. At Mass we are not simply remembering or reenacting—we are living in the present moment.

At Mass, then, we share in the Last Supper, the sacrifice of Calvary, and so we are in the presence of the real presence of Jesus, who gives us his Body and Blood, who gives us his life, which is eternal.

EIGHT

The Power of the Holy Spirit

It is all about presence. Maybe there is a crisis of presence in parts of the world today. There are different forms of presence that we did not have before. There is the virtual presence that was so beneficial during Covid. But the virtual presence can be the source of the crisis of presence today. There can be a lack of real presence in many homes today. The whole family can be physically present in the home, but they may not be present to each other. They can all be on their phones or whatever. This is not real presence.

However, the Mass is all about real presence. It is all about being present to God in all the ways that God is present to us. God's presence is both visible and invisible. In the Mass God is present. Jesus is present in his Precious Body and Blood. Holy Communion is not a symbol. It is the real presence of Jesus, the living presence of Jesus. There is nothing more sacred in the whole world and at any time than the Precious Body and Blood of Jesus on the altar and in the tabernacle. His presence is not virtual. It is real. Jesus is really and truly present. The Church is a sacred house. It is God's house, and God is present there in his Son, Jesus, who has given his life for us so that we can live, and live for ever.

Today our awareness and our belief in the real presence of Jesus in his Precious Body and Blood seems not to be as strong as it was in the past. Do we truly believe today that what we receive in Holy Communion is the flesh and blood of our risen Saviour? Do we truly believe that it is not just holy bread and holy wine? This is the Precious Body and Blood of Jesus: Jesus alive, present and living among us. The Council of Trent tells us that in the Most Blessed Sacrament of the Eucharist,

> The body and blood, together with the soul and divinity, of our Lord Jesus Christ and, therefore, the whole Christ is truly, really, and substantially contained.[19]

It is called the real presence because this is no fantasy or dream or wish or even virtual reality. We are not pretending here. We are not stepping out of reality. We are stepping more deeply into reality, more than we could ever fully image in this world. When we are in the presence of Jesus in the Eucharist we see and touch heaven. Heaven is more real even than earth because it is from heaven, it is from God, that earth was created. Sometimes faith and religion are seen as a flight from reality.

It is quite the opposite. They are an immersion in eternal reality. In fact, fleeing from religion, drifting from religion, abandoning religion, is a flight from reality. When we place all our hope in this world, it is fantasy and false hope. Our hope will disappoint us. When we immerse ourselves in the reality of God, most powerfully revealed in the Mass, our hope can never fail us, because Jesus is our hope. That hope is eternal. It is eternal because of what we celebrate at Mass. At Mass we celebrate the fact that Jesus has defeated death.

So how does this all happen? How does heaven enter earth at Mass? How does the bread and wine become the Body and Blood of Jesus? What happens? We don't see anything changing, but everything changes. So how does this happen?

It happens through the power of the word of Jesus and the action of the Holy Spirit. At the consecration of the Mass, it is Jesus who offers. It is Jesus who celebrates. It is Jesus who gives us his Body and Blood. The priest is in the person of Jesus, but it is not the priest's words, and it is not the priest's actions. It is the words and actions of Jesus. The words spoken at the consecration are not, "This is the body of Jesus," and "This is the blood of Jesus." No, the words spoken are,

> This is my body. This is my blood given up for you. (Matt. 26:26–28)

About the words of Jesus spoken at Mass, St Ambrose says,

> Could not Christ's word, which can make from nothing what did not exist, change existing things into what they were not before?[20]

The Word of God is the most powerful word spoken. In the book of the prophet Isaiah, God says,

> The Word that goes from my mouth does not return to me empty, without carrying out my will and succeeding in what it was sent to do. (Isa. 55:11)

When we celebrate the Mass, we are at the Last Supper. We are on Calvary. We are celebrating the Resurrection. We share in the life, the death, and the resurrection of Jesus when we celebrate the Mass. That is why our presence, our physical presence, is vital, if at all possible, at Mass. We need to be there. We need to be in Jesus and with Jesus. This is not virtual. This is real, and we need to be really present, just as Jesus is really present.

His presence in the bread and wine is as a result of his Word, his powerful Word, and also as a result of the Holy Spirit. The Holy Spirit is present and active at every Mass we celebrate. It is the power of the Holy Spirit entering the bread and wine that makes it the living Body and Blood of Jesus. The Spirit is the invisible presence of God at Mass. The Holy Spirit is the Lord, the giver of life. We have so much evidence of this in the history of the world.

When the angel Gabriel appeared to Mary in Nazareth and told her that God had chosen her to be the mother of his Son, Mary questioned. She asked,

> How can this come about since I am a virgin? (Lk. 1:34)

The angel Gabriel answered her,

> The Holy Spirit will come upon you and the power of the Most High will cover you with its shadow. (Lk. 1:35)

The Holy Spirit brought the life of God into the womb of Mary. She conceived Jesus by the power of the Holy Spirit. The Holy Spirit brought life, life eternal, the life of God. This is why we can profess our belief in the Holy Spirit, as the Lord, the giver of life, every time we pray the Creed. The conception of Jesus is not the only reason we can call the Holy Spirit the giver of life. The Holy Spirit gave life at another moment in the history of the world. St Paul tells us in his letter to the Romans that it is the Spirit who raised Jesus from the dead (Rom. 8:11). The Holy Spirit entered the tomb and gave life to the dead body of Jesus. We can imagine the Spirit, the dove of peace, entering the tomb and bringing life to the dead body of Jesus.

Always remember that Jesus rose in his body. This was not an out-of-body experience. Jesus was not a ghost when he rose from the dead. Jesus rose in his glorified body. While his friends may not have recognised him when they first saw him after the Resurrection, Thomas touched his wounds, and Jesus ate with them. We cannot touch the wounds of a ghost, and a ghost cannot eat real and solid food. So, the Spirit, the Lord, the giver of life, gave life to the dead body of Jesus in the moment of the Resurrection.

This is the same Holy Spirit who enters a person with the laying on of hands at their Confirmation. When the bishop or priest who celebrates the sacrament extends his hands over the person to be confirmed, he prays,

> All powerful God, Father of our Lord Jesus Christ, by water and the Holy Spirit you freed your daughter/son from sin and gave her/him new life.
> Send your Holy Spirit upon her/him. . . .[21]

The Holy Spirit is sent by God the Father, and the Spirit enters the person and is the source of eternal life. Therefore, we are temples of the Holy Spirit, and so our bodies are sacred, and we can live eternally with and in God. St Paul says,

> Your body, you know, is the temple of the Holy Spirit, who is in you since you received him from God. (1 Cor. 6:19)

It is the same Holy Spirit who enters the bread and wine at Mass. It is the Spirit who entered the womb of Mary. It is the Spirit who entered the tomb of Jesus. It is the Spirit who enters each one of us who is confirmed. The Holy Spirit enters the bread and wine. They receive the life of God and become the presence of God, God the Son, Jesus our Saviour.

In the Second Eucharistic Prayer the priest, after the "Holy, Holy," prays and begs God by saying,

> Make holy, therefore, these gifts, we pray, by sending down your Spirit upon them like the dewfall.[22]

The prayer is that the Holy Spirit permeates into the bread and wine just like the dew on the ground. It is a wonderful and beautiful image. As the priest prays, he has his hands extended out over the gift, the offerings. It is the same action as when the person is being confirmed. It is the laying on of hands. It is praying through our hands that God sends his Holy Spirit, the sanctifier, on the bread and wine so that they become the Body and Blood of Jesus. It is St John Damascene who said,

> You ask how the bread becomes the Body of Christ and the wine . . . the Blood of Christ. I shall tell you: the Holy Spirit comes upon them and accomplishes what surpasses every word and thought. . . . Let it be enough for you to understand that it is by the Holy Spirit that the Lord, just as it was of the Holy Virgin and by the Holy Spirit that the Lord, through and in himself, took flesh.[23]

This is God who is invisible revealing the visible presence of God—the one God. We do not see the Holy Spirit, but we do see the Precious Body and

Blood of Jesus. God is present, and he calls us to be present too. God is giving himself to us in his Son, in his Body and Blood, in the sacrifice of Calvary. God calls us and implores us to share in the life of Jesus and give ourselves to him, to offer ourselves to God.

After the consecration the priest prays in the Eucharistic Prayer,

> Humbly we pray that, partaking of the Body and Blood of Christ, we may be gathered into one by the Holy Spirit.[24]

The Holy Spirit who falls on the bread and wine like the dew, the breath of God who enters the bread and wine and makes them the Body and Blood of Jesus, is the person who unites us as one in Jesus as we receive his Body and Blood. Jesus gives his life for us on the altar of the cross so that we share in that life as one, united body, his body in the world today. We read in the Catechism of the Catholic Church,

> In every liturgical action the Holy Spirit is sent in order to bring us into communion with Christ and so form his body.
> (CCC 1108)

This is the heart and the fruit of the celebration of the Mass. At Mass we are called by God. God invites us to Mass. He calls each one of us by name to the altar. Before Mass in Confession, and at the beginning of Mass in the Penitential Rite, we empty ourselves of all that blocks us from God, our sinfulness. Then we are filled with God's Word. Then we offer ourselves with the bread and wine. As the bread and wine become the Body and Blood of Jesus, we are called to become the Body of Jesus in the world today, here and now. We are called to be in Holy Communion with one another. It is the Holy Spirit who gathers all those who partake in the Body and Blood of Christ into one.

This is one of the key reasons that we need to come to Mass. We cannot be Catholics on our own. Catholicism cannot be just a private devotional life. We cannot be the Body of Christ all by ourselves. It is the Holy Spirit who brings us together. This is not a virtual union. It is a physical union present in the Church. Our real presence is necessary to be the Body of Christ in the world today.

Jesus is really present at Mass. The Holy Spirit is really present. We need to be really present too.

NINE

In Holy Communion

Have you ever studied someone's face in a photograph? If you take time to do it, you notice things about their face that maybe you haven't noticed before. It might be the size or the shape of their nose. It might be their smile. You might recognise in a new way how much they resemble someone else, perhaps another family member. As you study their face you can be drawn into your emotion for that person. You can perhaps feel your love for them. If they have died you can feel a loneliness, a desire to see their face in reality again, to touch their face. That is the problem with a photograph. It catches a moment in time, but it is not alive. It can activate our memory, but it is about the past. The face is frozen in time. It may be a beautiful freezing, but it is frozen.

This frozen moment in time is in stark contrast to one of the most wonderful and exciting moments that there can be. That moment is at the airport, the explosion of love. Often it happens just before Christmas. Families are waiting for their loved one to come through the arrivals door. They have travelled from Australia or America or wherever, and often it is a long time since they were home.

The family might have brought a banner with them with words of welcome on it. Every time the door slides open there is the face of anticipation. Is this the moment? Sometimes it seems to take for ever, and they ask people coming through what flight they were on, to see if their flight has gone through security and baggage claim, and they wonder what is keeping them. Then the moment comes. There they are, face-to-face. This is no photograph. These are faces with tears of joy and smiles that are nearly too broad for the faces. Hugs are given. Faces are kissed and touched and caressed. This is pure undiluted joy, unbounded emotion, an explosion of love, a moment of light. There is certainly nothing frozen in time. This is no photograph. This is the present, living moment, and the future looks wonderful, and off they go to their home.

Face-to-face: In the Second Eucharistic Prayer, after the consecration, we thank God for holding us worthy to be in his presence and to minster to him.[25] At Mass, in the Eucharist, we are in the presence of God. Do we see him face-to-face? No, we don't see the face of God the Father. We are in the presence of God. God allows us into his presence, and he desires that we be in his presence. In God's presence we humbly pray that his Holy Spirit will gather us into one, gather us into the

Body of Christ. It is the prayer asking God to allow us to live in Holy Communion.

> Humbly we pray that, partaking of the Body and Blood of Christ, we may be gathered in one by the Holy Spirit.[26]

Then in the Eucharistic Prayer, those we pray to be with in Holy Communion are named. In the naming, and in the words used, the centre and the source of Holy Communion is revealed. This is so powerful, and it reveals why we cannot be Catholics on our own; it reveals why we need to be present with one another, really and physically present. When we come to Mass, we are present to one another in a way that the world cannot understand. It is real presence that is not confined only to those in the church with us.

The first group that we pray for that we are called to be in Holy Communion with is the Church throughout the world. When we are baptised, we become members of the Body of Christ, the Church, throughout the world. That means that we are the Church. We are one Church. We are called as the Church to reveal the love of God for the world. We are to be the love of God in the world. The love of God reveals the heart of God and the commandments of God. The reason

God's love reveals God's commandments is that God's commandments make us free. They make us pure. Purity leads to peace, and peace is at the heart of God. The Church that we are called to be, and we pray to be, is made up of human beings. It is led by the Pope, and in each diocese it is led by the Bishop. We are one body, united. St Paul says,

> Just as the human body, though it is made up of many parts, is a single unit because all these parts, though many, make one body, so it is with Christ. In the one Spirit we were all baptised. . . . (1 Cor. 12:12–13)

Yet the unity that we are called to live in the Church seems to be so easily attacked today. We even hear attacks on the Pope from within the Church today. In all the attacks that we hear there seems to be a consistent attitude that those who are attacking portray themselves as being superior and with superior knowledge. Our call to unity is a call to obedience. Obedience is always a challenge. It requires deep humility. In obedience we are called to engage in loving discernment, discerning where the Holy Spirit is leading us as a Church, as the Body of Christ. This is synodality, together, discerning where the Holy Spirit is leading us and how we are to preach the Good News to the world today and so to reveal the face of Jesus.

It seems to be so modern today to shrink our world to be the size that puts us at the centre and in control, so that what we want and believe becomes what drives the world. In this vein we hear today of people talking about their desire for a smaller, purer Church. If this is achieved the one thing for sure is that it is not Catholic and it is not from God or according to his plan. Jesus said,

> Go out to the whole world; proclaim the Good News to all creation. (Mk. 16:15)

Jesus also said,

> Put out into deep water and pay out your nets for a catch. (Lk. 5:4)

Jesus wants us to catch everybody in the net that is his Body. There is nothing small about God. His mind is eternal. He came to save the world. No one is to be lost. Jesus came to call sinners. In the Garden of Eden, the serpent managed to reduce the garden to one tree, the tree of the knowledge of right and wrong. When we believe we know better than everybody else, when our minds become small, we have eaten of the tree whose fruit we are forbidden from eating, and we have no further need for God. It is God who decides what is right and wrong, and he does that driven by pure love for us. We live in Holy Communion in the Church here on earth when we accept God's love and forgiveness and we love according to his commandments to love.

So, we are called to be in Holy Communion in the Church, not on our own, not lone rangers, not deciding ourselves what is right and wrong. As the Church we are called to spread out throughout the world, proclaiming Jesus at all times. Our focus is always to be on Jesus. Our Holy Communion is not confined to this world and to the Church made up of all God's baptised children here on earth at any given time.

As soon as we ask God in the Eucharistic Prayer to remember the Church spread throughout the world, we ask God to remember our sisters and brothers who have died. In this prayer for the dead, the source and the centre of our unity are revealed, and it is an eternal unity, the most wonderful source of unity. It is the most loving source of unity, the joy-filled source of unity. In the Second Eucharistic Prayer we pray,

> Remember also our sisters and brothers who have fallen asleep in the hope of the

> resurrection, and all who have died in your mercy: welcome them into the light of your face.[27]

The light of God's face is the source and centre of our unity, the source and centre of our eternal love, joy, and peace. It is the destination of our journey through this world if that is what we choose. This should be our aim in life and our only aim in life, to be welcomed into the light of God's face. This is what life is all about. This is no photograph or memory. This is the moment at the airport—only the moment at the airport is tiny compared to it. We have the opportunity, and we are called to see God face-to-face for ever in heaven.

That is what heaven is. Heaven is seeing the face of God. Imagine the emotion of God when we come through the gates. Imagine his embrace, his kiss, his tender touching of our face. Imagine his tears of joy. This is the emotion of heaven, and yes, even after death we journey. We continue our journey until our souls are so pure that they can see God.

> Blessed are the pure in heart. They shall see God. (Matt. 5:8)

Our hearts need to be completely pure to enter the gates of heaven and see the face of our God waiting for us to come home. At Mass we are in communion with those who are in the final stage of that journey through purgatory to the gates of our eternal home.

At Mass we get a glimpse of our eternal home. We are united. That is why it is vital that we are there, because we cannot truly say that we want to go to heaven when we die if we don't show any interest in heaven here on the altar while we live. When we come to Mass, we are united and in Holy Communion with our loved ones who have died and are on their final journey to see the light of God's face.

We are also in Holy Communion with those who have entered the gates of heaven and who are now welcomed into the light of God's face. We are in Holy Communion with Mary and all the saints in heaven. They are all together, the Apostles, the saints; everybody is there. The saints are seeing God face-to-face. Just imagine: They are there before him. The light of his face is shining upon them. There they are praising and adoring and glorifying God for ever.

So, we are in Holy Communion in three communities but always only one, the Church, because the Church is not confined to this world.

Yes, the Church is in this world, but the Church is also on the way to heaven through purgatory, and the Church is in heaven in the communion of saints. The Catechism of the Catholic Church speaks about the three states of the Church. It says,

> When the Lord comes in glory, and all his angels with him, death will be no more and all things will be subject to him. But at the present time some of his disciples are pilgrims on earth. Others have died and are being purified, while still others are in glory, contemplating "in full light, God himself triune and one exactly as he is":
>
> All of us, however, in varying degrees and in different ways share in the same charity towards God and our neighbours, and we all sing the one hymn of glory to our God. All, indeed, who are of Christ and who have his Spirit form one Church and in Christ cleave together. (CCC 954)

So, we are one. We are cleaved together in Christ. It is the light of God's face that joins us together. At Mass we celebrate and live the reality that we are not isolated. We are not on our own. We are united as one here, and on the way, and there.

This unity doesn't in any way diminish our individuality. Each one of us is a unique child of God who lives in the Body of Christ. Each one of us is a unique child of God, whose face shines upon us. We are not just a member of a group, but we are part of a body, just like a human body, as St Paul tells us (1 Cor. 12:12–30). Every part of the body is necessary and vital and unique. But every part of the body is lifeless if it is not integrated into the body. A leg on its own is not much use, nor is a hand or an eye. They need to be in the body.

When we stay away from Mass, we are separating the part of the body that we are from the whole body. That actually makes us lifeless. We are not in Holy Communion, because this is a physical Holy Communion. We are not in Holy Communion with our sisters and brothers in the Church on earth. We are not in Holy Communion with our loved ones who are travelling through the last part of the journey after death to the gates of heaven, and we are not in Holy Communion with those who have entered through the gates and are now seeing God face-to-face.

We need to be physically present and really present at Mass to show our desire to be physically present and really present in heaven. At Mass we can be with those in purgatory and those in heaven. Why would we not want to be with them now if we want to be with them for ever in heaven?

You see, God is waiting, but he is also here. Yes, when we die, we can see him face-to-face. While we live, we can receive his Precious Body and Blood into our lives so that we are united with him here and now on the way to heaven. This is the gift we have all the time. There doesn't need to be any loneliness even now when we see a picture of God or a picture of a saint or a picture of one on the way to be a saint. There doesn't need to be a separation. We don't have to rely solely on our memory. When the women went to the tomb on that first Easter morning, they went to remember and to care for what was. However, when they got there, they were told,

> He is not here. He has risen! (Lk. 24:6)

When we come to Mass, we reveal our belief in the Resurrection, and we reveal our belief that death is not the end. We reveal it in actions, not just words. By receiving Jesus, we live in Holy Communion with them all—Mary, the Saints, and those on the way to be saints, and we head towards the arrival gate of heaven, humbly confident that God our Father is waiting, and the light of his face will shine on us for ever.

TEN

God's Will Be Done

Me, myself, and I; my decisions, my rights, my life; it is all about me! Self-focus always seems to be a very strong attraction in life. In many ways we are encouraged to be self-focused today. It is my life, and I should be able to do with it whatever I want. We are encouraged to be independent and self-sufficient. We should not be relying on one another. Needing other people is perceived as weakness. Self-focus is really the foundation of selfishness.

It is very hard to be selfish and also be at Mass. It is very hard to be selfish and also to open ourselves to the mystery and the miracle of the Mass. Many people who don't go to Mass today give as a primary reason that they get nothing out of it. Often today in the Western world what we tend to be looking for from things is material gain or good feelings about ourselves. It is true that there is no material gain in going to Mass. Often it is true that our feelings may not change for the better because we are at Mass. Sometimes we can feel tired and impatient and even bored at Mass. To be aware of these feelings means we are focusing on ourselves. How am I? How am I feeling? How is the Mass making me feel? Suddenly it is all about me: me, myself, and I!

One of the shocking things about Mass is that it is not primarily about us at all. It is not about me. It is about God, Father, Son, and Holy Spirit. The fact that the Mass is about God is so powerfully expressed in the doxology at the end of the Eucharistic Prayer. The priest holds up the Precious Body and Blood of Jesus for everybody to see and he prays,

> Through him, and with him, and in him,
> O God, almighty Father,
> in the unity of the Holy Spirit,
> all glory and honour is yours,
> for ever and ever.[28]

The people respond by praying, "Amen!" The prayer is not through me and with me and in me. The prayer is not telling God that all glory and honour is mine. No, the prayer is about God. We pray to God the Father saying, "Through Jesus, and with Jesus, and in Jesus, O God, almighty Father, in the unity of the Holy Spirit, all glory and honour is **yours** for ever and ever." When we come to the end of the Eucharistic Prayer, we give all the glory to God and all the praise to God. It is God who makes us into one body. It is God who enables us to live in Holy Communion with the Church here on earth, the Church on the way to heaven after death, and the Communion of Saints in heaven. It is all God's doing, and all praise and all glory belong to him. It is not about us. It is about God. There is no place for selfishness at Mass. Selfishness and praising and glorifying God cannot coexist. That is not possible. The glory is for God. The honour is for God, and our source of unity is God.

So, at the end of the Eucharistic Prayer, we talk to God, our almighty Father, we honour him, we praise him, and we glorify him, and then we stand to pray. We pray the prayer that Jesus taught us. It is the prayer where Jesus gives us permission to call God our Father, Abba! Just think about the privilege and honour that Jesus gives us. Think of the intimacy that we can have and the love that we receive because we can call God our Father. We are so used to praying the Our Father that we can forget the relationship that we have been gifted with. Our almighty God, the creator of the whole world, is a loving and caring Father for each one of us. Just like all children, each one of us has a unique relationship with our Father. The Father that we have just praised and glorified for the Holy Communion that we live is the Father who we now talk to in the most intimate and childlike, simple way.

Jesus doesn't command us to call God our Father. He teaches us and he invites us, and he tells us that it is right that we do call God our Father. In the prayer that Jesus teaches us, the first thing we do after naming God as our Father is to reveal our belief in his presence in heaven. It is the face of God the Father that we will see if we arrive in heaven. That is where our Father is, and because he is our Father his name is holy. This reveals our call to be profoundly respectful of God. The one we glorify and praise in Mass is the one we are called to adore and hold his name holy and always holy. When Mary prayed the Magnificat in the presence of her cousin Elizabeth she prayed,

> The Almighty has done great things for me.
> Holy is his name. (Lk. 1:49)

Mary recognised the holiness of God's name, and we are called to do the same. The name of God is sacred. Imagine using your own earthly father's name as a curse. The thought of it is horrific. How much more horrific it is to use God's name in any disrespectful way. Imagine the pain of God when his name is so used.

In the Our Father we are speaking to the one who makes us all his children. Our focus is on our Father, and our prayer is again not self-focused. We pray that God's will be done. We are not praying that our will be done or that God agrees with the way we are doing things. No, we are praying that God's will be done on earth as in heaven. In heaven it is all God's will. In heaven as we see God face-to-face we are engulfed with God's love and God's peace and God's joy. On earth it doesn't have to be God's will. We have the freedom to do the will of the devil if we so choose. But in the Our Father we pray, no, we want our Father's will and only our Father's will to be done.

When we come to Mass, when we celebrate the Mass, this is the purest form of God's will on earth. In the Mass we share in the life of Jesus, in his body. We are sent out from the Mass to be the Body of Christ in the world. We are sent out with all that we need to do God's will. By coming to Mass, we surrender our will, and we accept and take on God's will. If we only want to do what we want and not necessarily what God wants, then Mass is a struggle. Yes, we can go for a while if we are looking for something specific; however, that motivation cannot last. We either get what we are looking for or we don't. When we are self-focused, Mass can be the clashing of wills. It can be so difficult to surrender our will for God's will, especially in the world today. It can't be about me. It has to be about God.

The prayer that Jesus taught us to pray to God our Father continues on to ask God for what we need, not for ourselves, but to do his will. We need our daily nourishment. We need to be forgiven, and we need to be protected from evil. Though the prayer is for us, it is not about us. It is not for material gain or to make us feel better. It is to free us to be able to do God's will more faithfully and truly. This radical other-focus can clash with the drive and the direction of much of the Western world today. The truth is that the drive to self-focus and ultimately to selfishness is the lure of the evil one. The tension that we can live in is revealed in the Our Father and the prayer after the Our Father. We pray to be delivered from evil.

Often today we don't think much about evil and about the evil spirit and the devil. Yet we pray in the Mass to be delivered from every evil. Why? So that we can have peace; the fruit of our freedom from evil is peace. Evil does exist and evil can take hold of us often in the most subtle ways. There is so much evidence today of the power of evil because there is so much evidence today of a lack of peace. Often today we can be led to believe that peace comes from self-focus. It is called "me time." This leads to a false peace that silences God in our lives. This is the subtle action of the evil spirit. Evil and peace cannot coexist. That is not possible. So we pray for peace.

In the Mass we pray for peace. Peace is not the absence of war. It is the freedom from evil. It is the freedom from sin.

Freedom is not something that we fight for; it is a gift that is given to us by God. God is the only source of true freedom. Freedom can only be found in our Holy Communion with God. Sometimes we believe that we can be free through amassing material things and being dictated completely by our feelings. This is a terrible trap to fall into, because it is not true. When we are driven by this world and by materialism and by self-focus, we are actually focusing on having, owning, and being in control. Then we try to use money and material things to give us security in life. This is the lure of evil, and it leads to false peace, to death, and ultimately to nothing. It leads us to the abyss of nothingness and profound insecurity. When we accept from God the gift of freedom, we can live secure lives that lead us to the fullness of life and peace. God is the source of our freedom, and God is the source of our security, and God is the source of our peace.

In the Mass after we pray for the gift of peace we speak to God, not now as our almighty Father, but as the Lamb of God. We speak to Jesus, the Lamb of God, and we ask for his mercy and we ask for his peace again.

The Lamb of God: There is something so tender and gentle and beautiful about a lamb. There is something so pure about a lamb. In the midst of the tension between evil and peace you would wonder about the power of a lamb. Why was it not the lion of God who could defeat all others on the world stage? The lion could be victorious. How could a lamb be victorious? Peace has to be fought for and won. Is a lamb any good at that?

It is wonderful that the Lamb of God appeared in Knock with Mary and Joseph and John in 1879. The Lamb is on the altar and the cross is rising from the altar. The altar is surrounded by angels. On the mosaic in the basilica in Knock depicting the apparition the lamb is so alert and so alive and so young and so free. This is a lively young lamb who could jump from the altar and run away. He was free. He wasn't tied. He was free. Yet Jesus, the Lamb of God, remained on the altar of sacrifice and gave his life to free us from sin. Jesus wasn't the lion who could dominate the world. He didn't have an army that could have secured him worldly victory and power. Jesus is the lamb who allowed himself to be sacrificed so that he could defeat the power of evil, of sin, which leads to death, and so that he could open heaven for us all.

That is what we share in the Mass. We don't come to Mass for worldly power and victory. We come to share in the life of Jesus, the young, free Lamb of God, who gave his life so that we can live for ever. So, when we come to Mass, we come to a sacrifice. We share in the sacrifice of Jesus. In other words, we give our lives, with Jesus, to God. The Mass then can never be about me, myself, and I. It is not about having or taking. It is about giving. It is in the giving that we receive.

This is why it is so important and vital that we come to Mass. It lifts us out of self-focus. It lifts us out of selfishness. It lifts us out of any desire for material security. It lifts us out of a focus on our feelings. When we enter into the life of Jesus and the sacrifice of Jesus, we are freed from evil and from the power of evil, and we receive the peace that can only come from the Lamb of God who takes away our sins.

ELEVEN

Absorbed into the Body of Christ

What happens when we receive? What happens when we receive the Precious Body and Blood of Jesus at Mass? Why did Jesus give us his flesh to eat and his blood to drink? Jesus talks very graphically about his flesh and blood. He says,

> The bread that I shall give is my flesh for the life of the world. . . . I tell you solemnly, if you do not eat the flesh of the Son of Man and drink his blood, you will not have life in you. Anyone who does eat my flesh and drink my blood has eternal life, and I shall raise him up on the last day. For my flesh is real food and my blood is real drink. He who eats my flesh and drinks my blood lives in me and I live in him. (John 6:51–56)

So, what happens when we receive Holy Communion? We receive the gift of life. We share in eternal life. We are given the gift of being raised up on the last day. When we receive Holy Communion, when we receive the Precious Body and Blood of Jesus at Mass, we share in the life of Jesus, and Jesus shares in our life.

What does all this mean? I think that it is important that we take it stage by stage.

> He who eats my flesh and drinks my blood
> lives in me and I live in him.
> (John 6:56)

We can understand how, when we receive the Precious Body and the Precious Blood of Jesus into our lives, Jesus comes and lives in us. He enters our physical being. We receive him into our bodies. This is a physical act. In some way when we receive Holy Communion, Jesus flows into every part of our being. This is the desire of Jesus, that there be no block, that there be no place that Jesus cannot flow into. It is the desire of Jesus that there be no place within our being where he cannot be. It is sin that blocks the flow of Jesus into our lives. That is why it is so important that we go to Confession, and it is why it is so important that we have the Penitential Rite at the beginning of Mass. We are removing all the blocks to Jesus's flowing into our lives.

When we receive Jesus, he wants to take over our lives. He doesn't want to be dormant in our lives. He wants to be free and alive within us. When we receive the Precious Body and Blood of Jesus in Holy Communion, Jesus doesn't want to be brought back to the restriction of the tomb. He wants to be free, and he wants to burst forth from our lives into the world. When Jesus lives in us, he wants to live in every room in our lives. He doesn't want anywhere closed off. Everywhere needs to be open so that Jesus can feel completely at home. If we are not willing to allow Jesus everywhere in our lives, we need to question if we should receive Holy Communion at all.

When we receive Holy Communion, Jesus comes to live in us, and we are not worthy. We acknowledge our unworthiness when after the Lamb of God is held up for us to see and adore, we say,

> Lord, I am not worthy that you should enter under my roof, but only say the Word and my soul will be healed.[29]

It is a wonderful admission to acknowledge that we are not worthy to have Jesus enter under the roof of our lives. It is so beautiful and it is so true. Of course, the first person we hear telling Jesus that he was unworthy to have him enter his house was the Centurion whose servant was dying. Jesus was coming to cure the servant when the Centurion sent the word,

> Sir, do not put yourself to trouble; because I am not worthy to have you under my roof; and for this same reason I did not presume to come to you myself; but give the word and my servant will be cured. (Lk. 7:6–8)

The Centurion's humility is incredible. He wouldn't even approach Jesus himself. He was so humble. This reveals how we should be as we come to receive the Precious Body and Blood of Jesus. We nearly should be led to the altar, daring not to look up. Receiving Holy Communion is never a right. It is always an undeserved gift. With this humility there is no way that we could block Jesus from going to any part of our lives. It would not be possible.

So, Jesus enters our lives when humility opens every door. Our body becomes his body. Our breath becomes his breath. Our hands and our feet become his too. In words attributed to St Teresa of Avila we are told,

> Christ has no body now but yours, no hands, no feet on earth but yours. Yours are the eyes through which he looks with compassion on the world. Yours are the feet with which he walks to do good. Christ has no body now but yours.

In some way we can understand this, but there is more to what happens when we receive. There is more to it than Jesus living in us, marvellous as that is. When Jesus is living in us, he is contained. In some sense we can believe that we have control of Jesus, that we can keep him to our size. Jesus would then fit in our lives. This cannot be the full story. We cannot reduce Jesus down to our size, to fit in us. That couldn't be right, and it is not. We know that it is not because of what Jesus also tells us. He says,

> He who eats my flesh and drinks my blood lives in me. (John 6:56)

How does this happen? How do we live in Jesus when we receive his Precious Body and his Precious Blood? What happens when we receive? What happens is so wonderful and beyond our imagination, and it is reveals the abundant nature of God. When we receive, it would be enough and more than we could ever expect that Jesus would make his home in us. However, there is so much more. We are called to make our home in Jesus. How do we do that? How do we come home to Jesus when we receive his Precious Body and Blood? The answer to these questions makes receiving the Precious Body and Blood of Jesus the profoundly radical act that it is.

Absorbed into the Body of Christ

When St Teresa of Avila speaks about our relationship with God, our union with God, she says,

> It is like rain falling from the heavens into a river or a spring; there is nothing but water there and it is impossible to divide or separate the water belonging to the river from that which fell from the heavens. Or it is as if a tiny streamlet enters the sea, from which it will find no way of separating itself, or as if in a room there were two large windows through which the light streamed in: it enters in different places but it all becomes one.[30]

What St Teresa is describing is a form of absorption where the little is absorbed into the great. St Bernadine of Siena, speaking about the joy of God, says,

> 'Enter into the joy of the Lord.' Although it is the joy of eternal happiness that comes into the heart of man, the Lord prefers to say to him 'enter into joy'. The mystical implication is that this joy is not just inside man, but surrounds him everywhere and absorbs him, as if he were plunged into an infinite abyss.[31]

This is what happens when we receive the Precious Body and Blood of Jesus. We enter into the life of Jesus. We are absorbed into the life of Jesus. We are dust, and we are reminded of this every Ash Wednesday with the words,

> Remember you are dust and to dust you will return.[32]

The dust that we are is absorbed into the Body of Christ. Without losing our uniqueness or our individuality we become members of this eternal, boundless Body of Christ. We are taken into the Body of Christ, and it transforms our lives, and we share intimately in the life of God. In Holy Communion we are plunged into the infinite abyss of God's light and life and love. When we receive Holy Communion, we receive our true and eternal belonging, and that is in God, in eternal light, eternal life, and eternal love. The dust that we are, God absorbs into himself. He envelops us into himself. When our bodies are placed in the ground and the clay is dropped on top of us, we are told,

> Dust you are and unto dust you will return, but the Lord will raise you up on the last day.[33]

When we receive the Precious Body of Jesus in Holy Communion, we are raised up. We are sharing in the Last Day, because we are sharing in God's time, eternity. Jesus says,

> Anyone who does eat my flesh and drink my blood has eternal life, and I shall raise him up on the last day. (John 6:54)

When we receive Holy Communion, we have eternal life. We are living eternal life now. That explains how the three states of the Church are united as one in the Mass. When we receive Holy Communion, we are present with the Church on earth. We are present with the Church in purgatory. We are present with the Church in heaven. We are one Church, united, here, there, and in heaven, all together, the one body.

In that one body the Precious Blood of Jesus flows within us, but more than that, like the body we enter into the Precious Blood of Jesus. The Precious Blood protects us. As we know, the Blood of the Lamb protected the household of the Hebrews in Egypt. They were passed over.[34] When we receive the Precious Blood of Jesus, we enter into his cascading Blood that enriches us and gives us his life and his energy here and now. The Blood of Jesus is full and rich, and it gives life to the Body of Christ. When we are absorbed into the Blood of Jesus, we are absorbed into his energy and his movement. If only the whole world were bathed in the Blood of Jesus, we would be protected and we would be safe.

At the offertory of the Mass the wine is put in the chalice and then a drop of water is added. The water represents the fact that Jesus was born as a human being into this world. The wine represents the fact that he is God. The water also represents us, our humanity. St Cyprian of Carthage says,

> Because Christ bore us all, in that he bore our sins, we see that by the water, people are signified, while in the wine, indeed, the blood of Christ is shown. And when the water is mixed with the wine in the cup, the people are made one with Christ.[35]

Just as you see the drop of water dropping into the wine, we are dropped into the enormity of the Precious Blood of Jesus. Just as we share in his body we share also in his life's blood. That is the gift of receiving Holy Communion. That is the gift of receiving the Precious Blood. We are not receiving wine. We are receiving the Precious Blood of Jesus. This was revealed to someone very powerfully who wrote about their experience of receiving the Precious Blood. The person said,

Absorbed into the Body of Christ

> When I consumed the Precious Blood at Mass today I began to anticipate the effect that alcohol has on me. It is the moment in the first drink when the impact of the alcohol is felt in my blood stream. It is that first moment of inebriation. I was blessed today to have a significant amount of the Precious Blood. I was in complete wonder and awe when I recognised that I didn't have any feelings of alcoholic inebriation. I realised that even in my weakest faith I knew there was absolutely no alcohol in what I had consumed. I realised then that the miracle of there being no alcohol left me with no alternative but to believe without any doubt that what I had consumed was the Precious Blood of Jesus.

This person received the most wonderful revelation about the Precious Blood of Jesus. That is truly what we receive. We receive the Precious Body and Blood of Jesus into our lives, and as we do, we are absorbed into the Precious Body and Blood of Jesus. This is what happens at Mass. This is what happens at Holy Communion. Therefore, nothing should stop us from receiving, because Jesus says,

> He who eats my flesh and drinks my blood lives in me and I live in him. (John 6:56)

Yet this may be one of the primary reasons that people struggle to practise their faith. The struggle doesn't come from not believing in God or in the Body of Christ, the Church. The struggle comes from knowing deep within themselves the enormity and boundlessness of God. That reveals our inability to control God or even to manage God. Many people cannot cope with this reality. Maybe it is no surprise that some people didn't come back to practise their faith after Covid. Covid made the world so small, and maybe we got a false sense of control within it. When we receive the Precious Body and Blood of Jesus, we surrender worldly control and enter into the enormity and the boundlessness of God. Many people cannot accept this, and so they reject this place of surrender. When we want to be in control of our lives, we cannot accept Jesus into our lives. His presence really is too challenging and maybe upsetting. It is the need to attempt to control our lives that leads us to distance ourselves from God and block God's entry into every part of our lives.

We need to come to Mass to let go of the myth of control and to surrender into the enormity and the power of God.

TWELVE

Powerful Medicine and Nourishment for the Weak

There once was a Parochial House that was burgled, and one of the items that was stolen was the tabernacle. In the tabernacle there was a small pyx with two Hosts in it. Fortunately, the key was not with the tabernacle, so the thief couldn't open it. Very shortly after the theft the thief was caught, and all that he had stolen was brought to the Police Station. The Police said that they would have to hold all of the stolen items for a period of time. However, they did agree that if someone went to the Police Station with the key for the tabernacle, they would allow them to take the contents away. This is what happened. A person went to the Police Station and opened the tabernacle, and the pyx was there, but when they opened it there was only the smallest particle of a Host in the pyx, not the two small Hosts that were expected to be there. The person searched the tabernacle, which was not too difficult to do because it was small with a curved reflective inside. The two Hosts were not in the pyx, nor were they in the tabernacle, just the small particle. So the person locked the tabernacle again, took with them the key and the pyx with the particle in it. They had to leave the tabernacle behind. One week later the owner was notified that he could collect his belongings from the Police Station. He collected the tabernacle and placed it on the front seat of his car, brought it back to the Parochial House, and put it back in its place. He then opened the tabernacle, and there in the centre of the floor of the tabernacle were the two Hosts, one with a small particle out of it.

This was incredible and miraculous. There was no way that the two Hosts could have been in the tabernacle when it was opened in the Police Station. Yet when the tabernacle was brought back to the house they were sitting plain to be seen, on the bronze floor.

This is a story that I know to be true because it was the Parochial House I was living in and it was my tabernacle, but I do not fully understand it. However, one thing that I believe from all that happened is that Jesus can take care of himself. At one level he decides where he is going to be or where he is not going to be. Therefore, we are not called to be his protectors. Jesus can protect himself. That does not mean that we should not take absolute care of the Blessed Sacrament and show the Blessed Sacrament absolute respect. Yet for some reason, I believe this is a relevant story when we are reflecting on who should receive Holy Communion and who should not.

The question about receiving Holy Communion can be a very political question and a very public question. It can cause great arguments and debates. It all seems very wrong. Fighting about Holy Communion, the Precious Body and Blood of Jesus, is so wrong. Nobody has the right to receive Holy Communion. It is always a gift that we are not worthy to receive. None of us is worthy to receive Holy Communion. So, who should approach the altar, who should be led to the altar, humbly, to receive the Precious Body and Blood of Jesus?

All sinners who confess their sin, and know their need for God, and accept his mercy should humbly be led to the altar, because there they will receive the heavenly gift of the Precious Body and Blood of their Saviour. There is no space for Jesus to enter the life of a person if they have not confessed their sins and accepted his mercy. Sin blocks Jesus in our lives.

We can have very technical debates about sin and mortal and venial sin. We can try to grade sins, one not being too bad or too serious. We can be comparing one sin to another. However, these debates often seem to ignore the effect of sin. The primary effect of sin is the pain that it causes to God. When we focus on the pain that God is experiencing, his crucifixion, because of our sin, then we don't want to commit any sin. You wouldn't think, *That's not too painful, so I'll do it!* We don't want to cause God any pain at all. Any pain is too much pain.

The first thing that eases God's pain is when we acknowledge our sins, when we accept that we have sinned, and when we name our sins—and more than name them, when it is our desire to be free from them. Often our movement from sin to freedom is a journey. Yes, God frees us every time we confess, but often we commit the sin again and again. However, our freedom always begins from acknowledging what we have done is wrong. Too often today what we seem to try to do is to convince God that what we are doing is right and that he is not up to date! We are trying to teach God about the modern world, and we are telling him that he needs to change! This is not the humility that is needed to truly receive the Precious Body and Blood of Jesus.

It is such a scandal that the altar becomes a battleground. The altar is the place of peace. It is the place of openness. It is the place of humility. It is the place of love. It is the place of communion, Holy Communion. Holy Communion is when we are completely one with Jesus. There is no separation. We are one.

Yet we are always on a journey to that oneness. We will experience an eternal oneness if we enter the peace of heaven. There we are one with God for ever. Here sin breaks that oneness. It prohibits communion. All sin prohibits real Holy Communion.

Today there can be a focus on some specific sins that prohibit Holy Communion, and it can be declared that those who commit them should be excluded from Holy Communion. In the very early centuries of the Church this was very simple to do, because all sins were publicly confessed to the community. The sinner was then excluded from the community until they completed penance. After completing their penance they were readmitted to the community, publicly again, for the Easter Vigil. When the public nature of Confession is removed, we have to tread very carefully in how we care for the public sinner. Their sin belongs in the Confessional with the guidance of the confessor. It is there that the truth of the sin and the context of the sin can be discovered. About the confessional Pope Francis said,

> I want to remind priests that the confessional must not be a torture chamber, but rather an encounter with the Lord's mercy.[36]

About the Eucharist Pope Francis said,

> The Eucharist, although it is the fullness of sacramental life, is not a prize for the perfect, but a powerful medicine and nourishment for the weak.[37]

We all need to receive Holy Communion, the Precious Body and Blood of Jesus. We need to receive. We need the heavenly medicine and nourishment that Holy Communion is. We need to have space in our lives for this medicine and nourishment. Sin fills us up with junk and poison. It is not the place where we want to bring the purity of Jesus. We need to get rid of the junk and the poison, and if it comes back, we need to get rid of it again and again and again. That is what Confession is for. That is what the Penitential Rite at the beginning of Mass is for. These are gifts, profound gifts to enable us to stop causing pain to God and to enable us to make space for Jesus in our lives.

It is very important, in a very particular way, for priests to realise this. You see, the one who sins does matter. I read two quotes recently that made this point very powerfully and clearly. St John Chrysostom says,

> The priest's wounds require greater help, indeed as much as those of all the people together. They would not have required greater help if they had not been more serious, and their seriousness is not increased by their nature, but through the dignity of their priesthood.[38]

As I read this I am reminded of the words of Jesus,

> When a man has had a great deal given him, a great deal will be demanded of him; when a man has had a great deal given him on trust, even more will be expected of him. (Lk. 12:48)

There is no doubt that a great deal is given to a priest, and a great deal is given to him on trust by God. To be the instrument of forgiveness in Confession, to be the hands that hold the bread and wine that become the Body and Blood of Jesus, to be in persona Christi, these are the undeserved gifts that priests are given. When they are so trusted, the pain that they can inflict on God is so much greater.

It all comes back to this. It comes back to God's pain. When we are all given the gift of the Precious Body and Blood of Jesus, it is the greatest trust that God can place in us. He trusts us with his Son. That is what we need to think about.

For those of you who have children, who would you trust your child with? It is a very small group, an exclusive group. That is wise and prudent. Who does God the Father entrust his child to? The answer to that question is *everybody*. God the Father entrusts Jesus to everybody. You can object and say that this is irresponsible and unwise. But is it? You see, God can entrust Jesus to everybody, in a profound act of wisdom and knowledge. The reason he can do that is because he knows each one of us better than we know ourselves. He knows our hearts. He knows our souls. He is in our souls. God knows that there is a sacred place within each one of us. It is the source of our love, the root of our love, the foundation of our love.

When we approach the altar to receive Holy Communion, the Precious Body and Blood of Jesus, we engage in an act of surrender. We surrender ourselves into the life and the love of God. As we do so, the love in our souls is unlocked. Jesus, in his Precious Body and Blood, unlocks the love of God that is contained in our souls. That is why God the Father entrusts his Son to everybody, because he wants everybody to have the love that is locked in their souls opened. The way to our souls is clear, and the way to the lock in our souls is clear when our sin is confessed and forgiven.

So, who should receive Holy Communion? All sinners on the road to heaven, all those who do not try to convince God that they are right and he is wrong, all those who clear the way to unlock the love of God in their souls, all those who want to live in pure Holy Communion with Jesus, these are the ones who should receive Holy Communion.

We are not called to protect Jesus. He can do that himself. We are not called to make the altar a place for political debate and fight. That is a scandal. We are called to surrender our lives humbly to God, because when we approach the altar we approach to give ourselves to God, and it is in the giving that we receive. We receive the Precious Body and Blood of Jesus, and so we enter into the embrace of Eucharistic Love that enables us to live in Holy Communion with God here and for ever.

THIRTEEN

Go Out in Holy Communion

What line in the Gospel makes you feel most uncomfortable? What is the line that challenges you most? For me the line is this:

> I tell you solemnly, in so far as you did this to one of the least of these sisters and brothers of mine, you did it to me. (Matt. 25:40)

Jesus says this when he is speaking about the Last Judgement. He is speaking about our eternal destination. He is revealing the fruit of our lives. If we spend our lives giving a drink to the thirsty, feeding the hungry, making the stranger welcome, clothing the naked, visiting the sick and those in prison, then when we die, Jesus will say to us,

> Come, you whom my Father had blessed, take for your heritage the kingdom prepared for you since the foundation of the world. (Matt. 25:34)

How we live in this world reveals where we go when we die. To those who do not give a drink to the thirsty, or feed the hungry; to those who do not make the stranger welcome or clothe the naked or visit the sick and those in prison, Jesus will say,

> Go away from me, with your curse upon you, to the eternal fire prepared for the devil and his angels. (Matt. 25:41)

This is dramatic language without any ambiguity. It is so clear, what we are called to do. This is how we live Holy Communion. This is why it is vital that we go to Mass and receive the Precious Body and Blood of Jesus and allow the Precious Body and Blood of Jesus to enter into every single part of our being and to surrender ourselves into the eternal Body and Blood of Jesus. When we are absorbed into Jesus we live in Holy Communion. When we live in Holy Communion, we recognise Jesus present in everybody else, and we minister to him. This ministering to others, this caring for others, this loving others, then, is not an unnatural, external action in our lives. It comes from our souls. It comes from the core of our being. It comes from Jesus alive in every part of us. It comes through the work of the Holy Spirit.

When we live in Holy Communion, we are one with Jesus. I read recently how someone described an experience they had, when they received the Precious Blood of Jesus, that reveals this oneness.

The person said,

> I became aware of the integration of Jesus' blood. It is more than integration because integration implies that it is two different physical realities joining together. The sensation was from the neck down. It was as if I had consumed nothing any different to myself. It was consuming myself, who I truly am. For me it was a most beautiful moment. I got absolute confirmation and certainty on this being the Blood of Jesus but more than this I got to fully experience being the Body of Christ.

We are not worthy to be the Body of Christ. It is a gift given us by God that reveals the abundance and the enormity of God and God's generosity. So, we are the Body of Christ. After the consecration of the Mass in the second Eucharistic Prayer we thank God that he has

> Held us worthy to be in your presence and minister to you.[39]

Then after Holy Communion, after receiving the Precious Body and Blood of Jesus, we are more than being in the presence of God—Jesus is present in us, and we are sharing in the life of Jesus. We are sent out as the Body of Christ; we are sent from the altar of the Word and the Sacrament to

> Go and announce the Gospel of the Lord.[40]

We are told,

> Go in peace, glorifying the Lord by your life.[41]

The Mass is an action. It is a living relationship. It is our relationship with Jesus, and it is Jesus's relationship with us. It is the celebration of Divine Friendship. It is the celebration of love and trust, and this love and trust are revealed in our being sent out to be the presence of Jesus in the world, to be the love of Jesus in the world. We are sent out to embrace the world with Eucharistic Love. We are called to embrace the world with our hearts and our eyes set on Jesus, on heaven. That is how we are to live in the world, because we have been to Mass. This is Holy Communion. To live in Holy Communion can be profoundly difficult. To share so completely in the life of another and to reveal the love and the gentle presence of Jesus to them can appear to be impossible. This is something that was revealed to me in a very powerful way.

In October 2006 I visited a prison outside Addis Ababa in Ethiopia. It was the most hopeless place I have ever been in. It was simply a field with a few mud huts in it. In the field there were about two hundred and eighty young men walking about purposelessly. Their spirits were so broken that they didn't even try to escape. They no longer dreamed of freedom. As part of our visit, we were brought into a mud hut which was their kitchen. It had no light except that coming from the opened door. In primitive and less than hygienic conditions bread was being baked for the prisoners. It was unleavened bread exactly like Holy Communion at Mass, only bigger. The chaplain, who was showing us around, lifted a piece of the bread, and he broke it and offered me a bit to try. I refused. I refused to share their bread, because I could not cope with their circumstances. I could not enter fully into the dreadful reality of their lives. I refused to be in communion with them. Afterwards I felt ashamed. I wanted to fix their reality, but I didn't want to stand with them in their reality—united with them as their brother. This was a rejection of Holy Communion by me.

In the Mass God is present in the Word proclaimed. There is heavenly power in Scripture, the power of the readings at Mass, the power of God's Word. It is his Word that flows through us and leads us to the altar, leads us to his presence in the Precious Body and Blood on the altar, that leads us to his presence in every person around the altar with us and in every person in the world who we are sent out to when Mass is ended.

For me this is one of the greatest challenges of the Mass. I believe in the presence of God in the Word. I believe in the presence of God in the Precious Body and Blood. It can be so much harder to believe in the presence of God in every other human being in the world. However, this is the challenging fruit of the Mass. This belief is the key to living in Holy Communion. This is what I failed to do in that prison in Ethiopia.

When we come to Mass, it is not to make contact with God as if he is beyond, out there somewhere, away in the east, beyond the gable wall. The messy truth is that God is here. He is present in the person in the pew beside you. He was present in every prisoner in that jail. Every human being is made in the image and likeness of God. Every human being has a soul. If every human being has a soul, then that means that

God resides in every human being. Whatever you do to the least you do to me, is what Jesus says.

So, when we celebrate Mass we cannot stay in a holy huddle isolated from the world in a place of protection and safety. That cannot be. We can never be content with smaller numbers attending Mass. Jesus sent us out to proclaim the Good News to the whole world, not just to those who we think want to listen or to those who we think are like us and would fit in. That is a contradiction to what we are celebrating, and it reveals that we are trying to restrict the size of God and the power of God and put him under our control. This is not right. We should never aspire to a smaller, purer Church. That is not the Church that is the Body of Christ. Nor should we want what one writer described as

> A moralising Church; a safe, immobile refuge from modernity which stands as a fortress against the world.[42]

The Body of Christ can never be reduced in size so that we become no more than a speck of dust. The Body of Christ can never be reduced in size so that the cascading Blood of Christ flowing abundantly over the whole world becomes a nice river flowing through nice places. We can never lose hope in the power of the Word of God, in the power of the Precious Body and Blood of Jesus, in the power of God alive in each one of us, in the power of the Church on earth, in purgatory, and in heaven. When we lose hope in that power, and when we believe that the power of the world and the power of the devil are greater than that power, we are restricting Jesus in us and us in Jesus. Who are we to try to control the Lord? We are never to be a fortress against the world but leaven in the world.

There is something very ironic about what happened in the Covid times. The unthinkable happened. Churches were closed. People couldn't physically gather as a community of prayer, as the Body of Christ. We could never have imagined the extremity that we had to face. People couldn't even gather to bury the dead, family members standing outside the closed doors of a church while the funeral of their loved one went on in the church. It was horrific.

However, we found ways. We discovered new ways. We couldn't be beaten, and we weren't. Look at what we did during Covid, how we thought differently and acted differently, because we had to.

Now when Covid for the most part is behind us, we seem to be too quick to admit defeat. Giving in to having fewer people come to Mass now and into the future is admitting defeat. Why can we not think differently and act differently now to bring people to the Church? It doesn't have to be this way. There is another way, and giving in to decline is certainly not God's way.

Each one of us has been given the gift of life from God. We have been given the gift of faith. With the gift of faith, we have been called to travel through this world along the Sacred Way, God's way, in the river of light and love being flowed along by the Word of God. We are nourished with the Precious Body and Blood of Jesus so that we are one with Jesus in Holy Communion, so that his light and his love shine through us as we journey to heaven, where Mary, the mother of God and our mother too, is waiting to welcome us home to the golden glory of the Resurrection. When we allow the light and the love of Jesus to shine through us, we will lead others onto the Sacred Way, into the river of light and love that leads us to heaven. We can never give up.

It is vital that we come to Mass and that we receive the Precious Body and Blood of Jesus, because without them it seems to be impossible to be sustained in the Sacred Way to heaven. How can you live in this world without sharing in the eternal life and love of Jesus? Why would you want to? Why would you want to even try?

The Precious Body and the Precious Blood of Jesus are the greatest gifts that you can possibly receive in this world. There is absolutely no better gift. All other gifts are confined and restricted by time, earthly time. They all pass away. It is only God who remains. Why would we not accept this gift? It is always there for us. Even if we are not travelling the Sacred Way in the river of light and love towards heaven, we can always start. It is the mercy and forgiveness of God that make the space in our lives for Jesus, and it is the mercy and forgiveness of God that draw us, that absorb us into his life, Holy Communion.

One of the great privileges a priest has is to take Holy Communion to those who are sick. I have had three wonderful experiences of taking Holy Communion to people who can longer come to Mass because of ill health and age. The first person cried when I placed the Host in their hand. The second person was overcome with joy and couldn't stop smiling and thanking God. The third person, when I held up the Host, crossed their arms over their heart and took a deep intake of breath. These people have profound faith in the real presence of Jesus.

Each one of us is called to pray for faith in the real presence of Jesus in his Precious Body and Blood. Pray for faith in the presence of Jesus in the Word proclaimed, and pray for faith in the presence of Jesus in all our sisters and brothers in humanity. When we believe in the real presence of Jesus, we will rebuild the Church and create a new world. We will be people of the Eucharist who will embrace the world with Eucharistic Love. We will give a drink to the thirsty, feed the hungry, clothe the naked, welcome the stranger, and visit those who are sick and those in prison. We will serve God and minster to God alive in everybody because we will live in Holy Communion with Jesus in the Church here on earth, in the Church in purgatory, and in the Church in heaven.

Why is it vital and necessary that we come to Mass? One word answers the question, and that word is the most sacred name ever uttered: Jesus.

NOTES

1 Sr Emmanuel Maillard, *The Hidden Child of Medjugorje* (Grude, 2007), 249.
2 https://www.pbs.org/wgbh/pages/frontline/shows/rwanda/todaniel/, accessed 15th August 2025.
3 *The New Jerome Biblical Commentary* (The Bath Press, 1993), 665.
4 Brian McCormick, *Homily for the Fourth Sunday in Ordinary Time*, Year C, 2022.
5 Pope Francis, *The Angelus*, 6th February 2022.
6 *Roman Missal* (Veritas, 2011), 380.
7 Message of his Holiness Pope Francis for World Communications Day, 24 January 2018.
8 *The Rite of Baptism for Children* (Veritas, 1992), 17.
9 Henri Nouwen, *You Are the Beloved* (Convergent, 2017), 97.
10 Pope Francis and Friends, *Sharing the Wisdom of Time* (Messenger Publications, 2018), 166.
11 *Roman Missal*, 416.
12 *Roman Missal*, 400.
13 *Order of Christian Funerals* (Veritas, 1991), 78.
14 The First Saturdays devotion was requested by Our Lady of Fatima, who promised "to assist at the hour of death with the graces necessary for salvation all those who, in order to make reparation to me, on the First Saturday of five successive months, go to Confession, receive Holy Communion, say five decades of the Rosary, and keep me company for a quarter of an hour, meditating on the mysteries of the Rosary."
15 Carmel of Coimbra, *A Pathway Under the Gaze of Mary, Biography of Sister Maria Lucia of Jesus and the Immaculate Heart* (World Apostolate of Fatima, 2015), 47.
16 St John Chrysostom, De prod. Jud. I, 6: PG 49, 380C.

17 Antonia Salzano Acutis with Paolo Rodari, *My Son Carlo* (Our Sunday Visitor Publishing Division, 2023), 66–67.
18 Fr Roberto Coggi, OP, www.miracolieucaristici.org.
19 Council of Trent (1551): DS 1651.
20 St Ambrose, *De myst.* 9, 50; 52: PL 16, 422-423. (CCC 1375).
21 *The Roman Pontifical* (ICEL, 1978), 77.
22 *Roman Missal*, 512.
23 St John Damascene, De fide orth. 4, 13:PG94, 1145A
24 *Roman Missal*, 515.
25 *Roman Missal*, 515.
26 *Roman Missal*, 515.
27 *Roman Missal*, 516.
28 *Roman Missal*, 516.
29 *Roman Missal*, 537.
30 St Teresa of Avila, *Interior Castle* (Dover Publications, 2007), 153.
31 St Bernardine of Siena, Sermon 2, on St Joseph.
32 *Roman Missal*, 70.
33 *Order of Christian Funerals*, 101.
34 Exodus 12:1–14.
35 St Cyprian of Carthage, Epistle 62, 13.
36 Pope Francis, *Evangelii Gaudium* (Veritas, 2013), 30.
37 *Evangelii Gaudium*, 31.
38 St John Chrysostom, *Six Books on the Priesthood* (St Vladimir's Seminary Press, 1984), 16.
39 *Roman Missal*, 515.
40 *Roman Missal*, 543.
41 *Roman Missal*, 543.
42 Christopher Lambe, *The Tablet*, 18 March 2023.

ABOUT PARACLETE PRESS

PARACLETE PRESS IS THE PUBLISHING ARM of the Cape Cod Benedictine community, the Community of Jesus. Presenting a full expression of Christian belief and practice, we reflect the ecumenical charism of the Community and its dedication to sacred music, the fine arts, and the written word.

SCAN
TO
READ
MORE

Learn more about us at our website:
www.paracletepress.com
or phone us toll-free at
1.800.451.5006

YOU MAY ALSO ENJOY

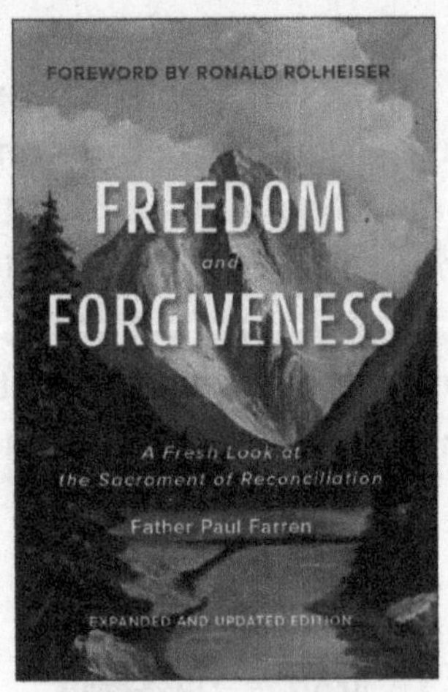

www.paracletepress.com